PENCOM INTERNATIONAL books are available at special discounts when purchased in bulk for premiums and sales promotions as well as for fundraising or educational use. Special editions can also be created to specification. For details contact PENCOM INTERNATIONAL at the address above. Thank you.

ISBN 1-879-239-12-4
1 — 7/96

Our sincere thanks to all the restaurant owners, operators and managers who contributed their valuable ideas to this book.

Graphics and design by Deborah Henckel and Katrin Luessenheide.

ALL FOR ONE

52 Ways To Build a Winning Team

by Andrea Stewart

CONTENTS

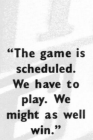

WINNING *IS* EVERYTHING

Whoever said "Winning isn't everything" never ran a restaurant. A drive down any street in America shows just how fierce the competition is in this industry. What are we competing for? A solid customer base is the trophy for which we all strive: People who come back again and again, bringing their friends. Winning customers is the only way to keep your doors open. It *is* everything.

"The game is scheduled. We have to play. We might as well win."

— Bill Russell, Hall of Fame Basketball Player

So how do you keep customers coming back? Give them the best quality food and the best quality service. "Easier said than done," agree most managers. But it can be done. You just can't do it alone. The problem is, winning customers is your goal, not necessarily your employees'. Most of them are just trying to get through their shift with a few bucks in their pockets. And you can't win without the help of your team.

Yep. There's that word again. Corporate America stole the teaming concept from the sports world a few years back, turning it into an abstract management ideal that would theoretically help companies succeed. And it worked. Those that have established team-oriented environments enjoy improved productivity, quality control and innovation of ideas.

A training exercise used to demonstrate the teaming concept to corporate executives begins by drawing an imaginary line between two people. The two players are told they win if they can verbally convince the other person to cross the line. Before teamwork training, players almost never convince the other. But after learning how to trust each other, communicate well and work toward a common goal, team players simply say, "If you'll cross the line, so will I." They exchange places and they both win. *That's* teamwork.

But convincing restaurant workers to cross that line has been a little tougher because corporate America's abstract teamwork theories don't really apply in the hustle and bustle of the typical restaurant. Managers rant and rave about "acting more like a team," but they can't show their employees how.

You've seen the consequences when staff don't work together effectively: Mistakes are made, customers are treated rudely with hasty remarks like "sorry, not my section," fights break out between front-of-the-house and kitchen staff, employees who resent being thrown into "the weeds" by others' disorganization conspire to bring others down with them. Morale drops, service suffers and the overwhelming sense of chaos makes your restaurant a less-than-desirable place to be. And it's your customers who will feel it first. When they decide not to return, you lose.

This book clarifies those abstract teaming theories and shows you how to put them to work in your restaurant operation: Choosing the right team players, developing strategic team plays, coaching members to use their individual skills for the benefit of the team, motivating the team to outperform the competition and showing your people how when the team wins, *they* win. It's all in how you play the game.

HOW TO USE THIS BOOK

We've broken the book down into four chapters:

Chapter One, "Building Your Team," will show you how to start. First you'll learn why teamwork is so important in restaurants. What does it look like when it works? What are the consequences when it doesn't? Here's where you'll begin to build your strategy for a team-oriented environment in your restaurant – recognizing *your* role in the team-building process, improving morale, changing policies and procedures to support team play, hiring and maintaining the best team players, setting goals and communicating those goals to your staff.

Chapter Two provides a "Play by Play" on how to put teamwork theories to work in the typical restaurant. We'll discuss how to choose leaders and schedule shifts for the best team performance. We'll break down restaurant positions to describe each employee's role on the team. And we'll show you how special teams can help you solve your operation's biggest problems.

In Chapter Three, "Practice Makes Perfect," we'll discuss why you can't just say, "We need to act more like a team." A team environment requires layer upon layer of trainable skills like communication, trust and accountability. We'll explore effective training techniques such as mentors and cross-training, and we'll talk about some more advanced team-building concepts like managing conflicts and problem solving.

And in Chapter Four, "Going for the Goal," you'll learn how to encourage teamwork by rewarding employees for their participation in a team environment. Team-building compensation is a whole different attitude for restaurants since servers are used to being tipped for their individual performance and singled out for high sales while kitchen staff and management are often paid the same no matter how good their performance. These practical (and a few radical) ideas will help you tie pay to the performance of the team.

Each of the 52 ideas is presented alongside a variety of related tips, techniques, samples, lists, inspirational quotes and incentive ideas. The complete package will provide you with a team-building strategy that you can put to work in your operation. The ideas are presented in easily digested sections to help you read and absorb them one at a time.

The wealth of great ideas in this book can apply to all types of operations – from fine-dining and casual-theme restaurants to quick-service and pizza joints. Granted, not all operations are alike. What works for your place may not work for the one down the street. Take the ideas you like, and leave those not to your taste here in the book.

Once you've finished reading, you can implement these ideas by turning to the Action Plan in the back (page 118) and the subsequent Strategies (pages 119-120).

"Managing is getting paid for home runs that someone else hits."
— *Casey Stengel*

CHAPTER ONE:
Building Your Team

Introduction

Who's the most valuable player on a team? Well, by definition, every team member is essential to its success. But in the beginning stages of team development, just one person stands out – the coach.

As manager and leader of your restaurant's staff, it's up to you to build the framework for a team culture.

The best place to start is by understanding why teams are so important in restaurants. What are the consequences of a staff that doesn't work together effectively? Lost profits through lost customers. But you probably realize those consequences every day. What you don't see is what teamwork looks like when it's working. And once you've seen it, you won't want to go back.

On the pages that follow are 14 great ways to help you begin to build your restaurant team. First you'll hear what Webster has to say about teams – it's probably not what you'd expect. And you'll get a glimpse of a typical restaurant through the customers' eyes – first of teamwork gone wrong, then of teamwork "in a perfect world." And you'll learn how to recognize *your* role in the team-building process, create an environment that supports the team, choose the best players and persuade those players to use their individual skills for the benefit of the team.

By Definition

Defining "teams" and "teamwork" for restaurants

You've heard it – or maybe even said it – so many times that the mere mention of *team* can be perceived by your staff as nothing more than lip service. You can almost hear the empty promise: "Sure, coach, I'll pitch in for the team." Yeah, right. In this business, too often it's every person for him or herself. Clock in. Pocket the tips. Call it a night.

Part of the problem is that the word "team" means something different to everyone you try to coach into participation. Think about your own definition. Do you believe that any group that works together is a team? Not always. Another misconception is that "teams" and "teamwork" are synonymous. Sure, they're related, but "teamwork" more appropriately describes behaviors that can help individuals and organizations as well as teams: listening to others, responding constructively, giving others the benefit of the doubt and supporting people who need support.

So if a team isn't just a group of people, and it isn't people practicing "teamwork," then what is it? *A team is a small number of people with complementary skills who are committed to a common mission for which they hold themselves mutually accountable.*

Let's break the definition down for further understanding:

1. Small number. Most successful teams have two to 25 members. A larger number – say, your restaurant's entire staff – will have difficulty interacting and making

decisions. Ten to 15 people find it easier to work through their differences toward a common goal. Your best bet is to think of your restaurant as a series of related teams: front of the house, kitchen, management and a variety of sub-teams.

2. Complementary skills. Successful teams require three types of skills and knowledge: *Technical expertise*. They have to first be able to get their own job done. *Problem-solving and decision-making skills*. They must know how to evaluate problems, plan strategies and make decisions. *Interpersonal skills*. They need to be able to state their opinions clearly, listen actively and provide helpful suggestions.

3. Common mission. Each member's immediate tasks must relate to the team's overall purpose. If short-term objectives don't match the long-term picture, team members will feel confused and discouraged.

4. Mutual accountability. A group becomes a team only when it can hold itself collectively responsible.

TIP   Benefits of Teamwork

Now that you know what it is, here's what you can expect improved teamwork to do for your operation:

- **Greater productivity**
- **Effective use of resources**
- **Better-quality products**
- **Increased customer traffic**
- **Higher-quality decisions**

- **Improved customer service**
- **Improved problem solving**
- **Creativity and innovation**
- **Improved staff relations**
- **Increased profitability**

2 Sound Familiar?

What bad teamwork looks like

> **"Sometimes you need to look reality in the eye, and deny it."**
> — *Garrison Keillor*

It was a decision Emily Franklin would soon regret: The commercial for Joe's Bistro came on while she wondered where to take her parents for their anniversary tonight. "That's it!" she said.

Her first clue came as she, her brothers and parents filed into Joe's busy entry. Julie, Joe's star server, scurried through the crowd without a word. Peter growled at the guests in his path as he juggled his overflowing bus tub. Heather rushed back to the greeter stand. "How many?" she asked frantically. "Seven," Emily replied. Heather groaned, then glanced over at the two empty four-tops in Julie's already busy section. She thought, "So, she wants to blame *me* for not making enough in tips last night? I'll show her." She barked at Peter to pull the tables together. "Right this way."

From the back office, Joe couldn't tell how well his new commercial was working to bring in new guests. He looked over his P&L statement. "How are we going to make it?" he wondered. "Maybe another ad. Or a sales incentive – that'll keep 'em going."

Julie loved to sell, but hated the grunt work. Other servers said she would make a great used car salesman. But her overly pushy sales skills didn't win a lot of repeat customers. Tonight she would sell the Franklins on premium cocktails, appetizers, a bottle of wine and steaks all around. "Oh, and some water and silverware?" asked Emily. "Sure. Soon as I find that buser," said Julie.

Neither had arrived when the appetizers did. Julie had forgotten to tell Peter. But that didn't matter since Peter was busy in the back arguing with the dishwasher over a broken glass. "And our drinks?" asked Emily. "Damn you, David," Julie muttered, looking toward the bar. "Somebody'll bring them right over."

Meanwhile, tempers in the kitchen were heating up. "Oh, man," said Curtis at the broiler when the bundle of orders arrived. But rather than get through them one by one, he held them and passed all the orders on to the new expediter together. "If I'm getting slammed, he's going down with me," thought Curtis. "He needs to learn how things *really* happen back here."

Emily's steak was over-cooked. "Could you take this back to the kitchen?" she asked the nearest server. "Sorry," said Pam. "Not my section." Five minutes passed before Julie's return. "Are you *sure* you ordered medium rare?" she asked, double-checking her ticket. "Oh, so you did." She stormed into the kitchen: "You guys screwed up another one. Medium rare this time – and make it quick!"

Emily balked when she saw the check total, then set out her credit card on the corner of the table amid the dirty dishes. Busy servers and busers ignored it as they rushed by. Julie was nowhere in sight. Finally Emily flagged down an assistant manager. "Julie? I think she's on break. I'll try to find her for you."

TIP

Epilogue

Julie was furious with Heather for throwing her into the weeds. But since the Franklin party was large, its gratuity was automatically included so she still came out with a healthy take for the night despite all the unhappy guests. And besides, she won the award for high sales that month. When Julie walked up to accept her cash at the staff meeting, a collective groan could be heard from the audience. "Funny how we do all the work and she makes all the money," whispered Peter. From the back office, Joe frowned as he scanned his P&L again. Emily grimaced the next time she saw the commercial for Joe's Bistro. "Yeah. Fat chance," she said.

3 In a Perfect World

What good teamwork looks like

> "Understanding how to operate a successful restaurant is a lot like having a hangover. Until you actually experience it, you just don't know what it's like."
> — *Diamond Jim Brady, 1902*

Saturday afternoon, Joe stood back, proudly surveying his restaurant. Since implementing a team strategy, he'd seen profits jump nearly 30 percent and all that positive word-of-mouth advertising had eliminated his need for TV commercials. Tonight they expected to be especially busy and his shift leaders were preparing their teams in pre-shift meetings.

Julie stood before the front team, running through a quick sales training session. "OK, everyone, tonight's focus is on appetizers and Joe's promised us a bonus if we can increase each of our averages by two. Pam, you had a great night last night. How'd you do it?" Joe headed to the back where Curtis was leading the team through a quality-control session.

Several of Emily's friends had recommended Joe's Bistro as the perfect spot for her parents' anniversary dinner. She sensed when they entered that they were in for a great experience. Julie passed by with a smile. "Hi, folks. Heather will be right with you," she said, signaling to Heather. Peter went to pull two tables together as Julie ran his bus tub to the back. She stopped in the kitchen to say, "Hey, guys, things are starting to heat up." Pam's section was still empty, so she went to the bar to warn David about the rush and ask if he needed extra garnishes from the kitchen, then she went to prepare silverware rollups.

In the back, Curtis was helping the new expediter prepare for his first shift. "When things get hectic, don't be afraid to call for help." Things did get hectic, so when Curtis had a break between orders at the broiler, he went to help out.

Julie came back with an over-cooked steak. "Hey, guys, I know you're busy, but the guest would prefer medium rare. Would you mind rushing it?" "No problem," said Curtis. When the new platter got to the food runner, Curtis told him: "Top priority, please, and delivered with apologies."

Back on the floor, Julie surveyed her section. Everyone had what they needed, so she headed to Pam's which had filled up quickly. She signaled to Pam who was rushing to the bar with a drink order. "Table four is at C&D," said Pam, relaying the code for coffee and desserts. At table four, Julie said, "Hi, folks. Pam will be right back to check on you, but she asked me to tell you about our dessert selections ... " Peter was filling waters at Emily's table. "Could you find our server?" asked Emily. "My father would like another drink." Peter replied, "Oh, I'm happy to get that for you. Gin and tonic? Would you like to try Bombay in that?"

Joe smiled as he passed through the room, thinking about his P&L. But those thoughts quickly vanished when he saw Emily place her credit card and ticket on the corner of her table. "How was everything tonight? Food prepared just the way you like it?" he asked, picking up the check. "Yes, it was great," Emily replied. "I'll have this back to you in just second," said Joe. "Hope you'll be back to see us soon."

"We will," said Emily with a smile.

TIP

Measure for Measure:

Does the preceding scenario describe a typical night at your restaurant? Most would admit no, but ask yourself how many of the following "characteristics of an effective team" are true of your teams to see how well you measure up:

- **Clear roles and work assignments**
- **Shared goals**
- **Open communication**
- **Consensus decisions**
- **Trust**
- **Shared leadership**

4 The Customer Connection

Create an atmosphere where guests want to come back

Ever wonder if your staff's in-fighting, disorganization, communication breakdowns and low morale are affecting your customers? Stop wondering and accept it: You can't hide that negativity from the people who visit your operation. In fact, your guests probably notice those problems more than *you* do. A lack of teamwork means slower service, more mistakes, rude staff and negative dining experiences.

Still, many operations ignore their internal problems while throwing money at marketing schemes to get more customers through the front door: television advertising, expensive promotions, big banners outside.

Some advice: Don't waste another dime on advertising until you can improve the competence of your restaurant's staff. Sure, your external marketing efforts build new traffic, but once customers experience that bad service in person, they'll never return. If bad service drives them away, no amount of advertising will motivate them to come back. And they'll tell their friends not to visit your place, either. That one step forward has brought you three steps back.

What does that mean to your bottom line? Say your average guest check is $12 and you lose four customers per day through poor service. That's an annual loss of $17,520. Ouch! And that doesn't even include the number of people who won't visit your place because of negative word-of-mouth advertising.

Take your advertising budget and invest it in improving your restaurant's staff. By fostering a team-oriented environment and training staffers to be team players, you'll see improved communication, better quality products, higher morale – and most important, the kind of customer service that will turn a first-time guest into a regular.

We're talking about *internal marketing*. It's the quality of service that makes people glad they came to a restaurant, makes them want to linger a little over an after-dinner drink or dessert they may not have originally planned on, and makes them want to return often – with their friends. One step forward – a little time and training – brings you three steps *further* by encouraging increased sales and repeat customers, which are the best kind you could want.

What's Your Problem?

A lack of teamwork hinders communication, often when it's most needed. When guests have a problem with their meal or service, for example, sometimes all they want is someone to listen. The trouble starts when they have to explain the problem over and over, only to hear, "Sorry, not my section" or "I'll get the manager," who says, "What seems to be the problem?" They begin to wonder if they're in an episode of the *Twilight Zone*. One of the simplest ways to show customers you care is to encourage staffers to listen and try to take care of the problem themselves – no matter whose section it's in. If they absolutely have to go to a manager, they should explain the guest's problem in detail. The manager can then approach the table knowing all the information: "Sir, I understand there is a problem with your check total. How can I fix it?"

5 It's Up to You

The manager's role in team-building

> "A man should first direct himself in the way he should go. Only then should he instruct others."
> — *Buddha*

Teamwork doesn't happen by accident. People aren't born to be team players. And from the youngest of ages, Americans are trained to be competitive rather than cooperative. That's why you can't just say, "We need to act more like a team." Your people won't know where to start. It's up to you, the manager, to show them. Only you can effect the changes you want to see in your operation. Your role is head coach, and here are your responsibilities to the team:

Start by building an "Action Plan" which outlines the steps you'll need to take to improve teamwork in your operation. In planning for the future, the first step is to take a look back. A hard look. How effectively has your staff worked together in the past? What's going wrong? Do policies and procedures hamper or encourage a team environment?

Visualize your people working together more effectively, and make a list of areas that need to improve to make it a reality. Use the list to develop strategies for achieving that ideal. This book will help you with many of them, but tailor the strategies to your operation, your people.

Be prepared to "say the right words" and make them come alive every day. Many organizations adopt a vision statement or a list of values. These statements usually call for teamwork, quality, customer service and other admirable goals. Statements are necessary but not sufficient. If you want team play to be a way of life, examine every important decision you make in light of its impact on the team.

Incorporate the team-player concept into all polices and procedures: training, scheduling, hiring, salary reviews, bonuses, incentives, etc.

Act in ways that support team players. When performance appraisals, salary reviews and promotion decisions are made, weigh team-player accomplishments equally with task accomplishments. And when rewards and recognition are distributed, acknowledge team players in ways that demonstrate the importance of teamwork to the success of the operation.

Most important, ask yourself if you're a part of the team. You may be the head coach, but you will be expected to don a jersey now and then. When your employees see you coming, do they say, "Here comes help!" or "Here comes trouble!"? When a dishwasher doesn't show up for a shift, are you screaming at the other dishwashers to pick up the pace, or are you dipping your hands in to get the job done? You set the work atmosphere as manager and leader – and your employees will follow that lead.

Leading by Example

For you, the challenge is to be the best possible team player. This means many things.

- **Knowing your style, including strengths and your potential for ineffectiveness.**

- **Developing a plan to optimize your strengths and minimize your shortcomings.**

- **Being aware of your team's stage of development and what they need from you during each stage.**

- **Acknowledging that your employees will have different styles. Be willing to work with others to see this diversity as a team strength.**

6 Mission: Possible

Setting your operation's mission and goals

"First we will be
best, and then we
will be first."
— *Grant Tinker*

If you don't know where you're going, you probably won't wind up there. Before you can build a team environment, you must first decide on the team's mission – where do you want it to go? What do you want it to do? By defining a clear "team mission," you show employees their place in the big picture. And by outlining goals to help them achieve the mission, you give them something to shoot for together.

But not so fast. Defining a team's mission and goals is a five-step process:

First define your *operation's* overall "mission." What are you in business for? Well, let's be honest ... it's to make money. While everyone wants to believe they're in business to provide a product or service that customers need, there probably isn't a company on the planet that isn't in it for financial gain. So your operation's mission is to be profitable. How do you do that? For most restaurants, it's by minimizing waste while providing guests the best quality food and service to keep them coming back.

Use the operation's mission to define a mission – or purpose – for each team. A team without a common mission will wander from task to task despite the best team-building efforts.

What's the team's mission in helping the operation be profitable? The front-of-the-house team's mission may be "Selling more food and drink while providing guests with a quality dining experience that encourages repeat visits." The kitchen team's mission may be "Reducing waste and providing guests with a consistently good meal that encourages repeat visits." Notice that a team's mission differs greatly from its goals. A mission should have a "pie-in-the-sky" quality – something they'll have to continue to strive for every day.

When you begin to build your teams, ask for their help in defining the problems that keep them from achieving their mission: What specific hurdles keep profitability low and prevent customers from coming back? Inconsistent quality, poor service, an unclean dining room, waste in the kitchen, etc.

Now have members use those problem statements to develop a list of do-able team goals, like "Increase sales," "Minimize mistakes," "Provide great service" or "Reduce waste." Work together to attach milestones to each. For example "Reduce mistakes by 10 percent in the next month." Or "Increase sales by 10 percent in the next month." Or "Minimize customer complaints by 10 percent in the next month."

Putting Goals to Work

How do you motivate employee team members to "go for the goal"? It depends on the goals. You'll have the most success if goals are:

Stated positively

Specific and concrete

Realistic and attainable

Measurable

Set with the cooperation of the people involved.

7 Environmentally Sound

Create an environment that supports teamwork

You may not know it, but the root of your problems in building teamwork might be found in your own policies and procedures. If the organizational norm is "do your own thing" or "be the best of the best," then staffers may think working together as a team is not valued. Create an environment that supports teamwork by scrutinizing policies and procedures to eliminate team-busting practices.

Never rank your employees. By referring to your "top server" or "top cook" at meetings, you give other employees the impression that they make up "the bottom." It creates competition to be Number One. And why would the other employees want to help Number One to stay there? And what would Number One gain by helping out someone else? He or she has already earned your acceptance, so there's nothing left to prove.

Don't award promotions "in title only" with no new responsibilities. Some managers do this when they want to recognize good performers with a raise, but the budget won't allow it. Handing out a new title to one member of the team will further segregate employees, especially if they're all performing the same responsibilities.

Make raises and promotions a cause for celebration, especially if they're awarded for exceptional performance on the team. When you deem an employee worthy of a few extra bucks in his or her paycheck, tell the rest of the staff why: "Susie never misses a chance to help out everyone on her shift – and she never fails to complete her own tasks in

> **"You can take great people, highly trained and motivated, and put them in a lousy system, and the system will win every time."**
>
> — *Geary Rummler, President, The Rummler-Bache Group*

the process. She has strived to achieve the team's goals and for that, we wanted to recognize her with a 25-cents-per-hour wage increase." Or award small wage increases or bonuses to everyone on a team for working together effectively and meeting their team's goals.

Sales incentives are great for boosting revenues, but while you're trying to build teamwork, you may want to revisit your incentives with a team approach in mind. Incentives that single out "top sales" motivate servers to do nothing more than sell. When their eyes are on the prize, they may see nothing else. That means other responsibilities fall by the wayside. Other employees, who won't be rewarded for their efforts, often have to pick up the additional responsibilities. Resentment grows, and efforts toward building teamwork are destroyed.

Outline all of your policies in an employee handbook so that employees are on the same page. In your handbook, be sure to include a "vision statement" that outlines your operation's philosophy and commitment to creating an environment that fosters teamwork. Refer to those philosophies as you explain policies. It will explain the "why" along with the "how."

Character Study

Here are the characteristics of an environment that supports teamwork:

The atmosphere tends to be informal, comfortable and relaxed, with no obvious signs of boredom or tension. Members feel comfortable speaking with each other regardless of position and enjoy being around each other. They look forward to contact with other team members. Humor is an integral part of successful teams. A team with a positive climate ignores formalities like voting and raising hands before speaking. Rather, an obvious ease of interaction and communication relaxes members. In a relaxed, informal environment, people feel free to engage in good-natured kidding, social banter about events unrelated to work and anecdotes regarding recent company business.

8 The Dream Team

Hiring team players

"Superstars need not apply," should be your recruiting philosophy if you want to build a team-oriented operation. While everyone says they're "good with people," it takes a different type of person to help you build your dream team.

So when hiring, look for applicants with a good "team" attitude, not just technical skills. Ask applicants if they participated in any team sports in high school. And ask them to describe their role on the team. Watch out for those who respond: "star player." They may always want to be singled out.

Look for employees with a high degree of pride – those who wouldn't dream of walking past a piece of paper on the floor or letting the phone ring off the hook. Seek people who will bring high energy and excitement to their jobs, qualities that indicate they welcome a challenge.

Search for people who communicate well and have the confidence to be open to suggestions and constructive criticism. Ask them behavior-based questions, such as "Can you describe a situation in your previous position when you had to deal with a conflict with a co-worker?" "How did you handle it?" "What would you do differently?"

Look for people who understand it is their responsibility to get better at their job so they require less help and have the ability to pitch in to help when others get busy.

> "You don't try to build character in a team, you eliminate people who don't have character."
>
> — *Paul Brown, Cleveland Browns founder*

Once all your teams are formed, don't damage them by forcing someone who doesn't fit into the picture. Instead let your team leaders interview applicants and help with the hiring decision. And get second opinions from the rest of the staff. When that candidate came in to fill out an application, how did he or she treat your greeter?

Make it a part of the interview process to take applicants on a restaurant tour. Introduce them to as many employees as possible – especially the teammates they'd be working with. Give them a chance to chat. Coach employees beforehand on conversational questions they should ask. Create a form to pass out to every employee who meets the applicant. It doesn't have to be anything fancy, just ask if the candidate was pleasant, respectful and, "Was this someone *you* would want to work with?"

Don't base your final decision on any one employee's opinion. Rather, take them all into consideration. Your existing employees will be happier and your new employees will stay longer.

Birds of a Feather

Once you've hired four or five good people, hire their friends. Forget the outdated advice "never consider friends or family for hiring." This makes no more sense than hiring people based only on age, gender, ethnicity or schooling. Good people are good people. And when you hire a group of people who know each other, much of the team-building is done for you. In a friendlier environment, staff will help one another get the job done – and not because they have to. You'll decrease the number of staff conflicts. And you'll end up with a solid team made up of similar personalities. To help promote this environment, post job openings internally and get your staff to help you recruit by offering a bounty for referring their friends. For instance, if a server recommends someone for an open position, and that new hire stays at least 30 days, give that server a reward for the referral.

9 In Style

Know the four different team-player personality styles

Each member of your staff has the capacity to be an effective team player, but in different ways. There are four types of "team-player personality styles," each contributing to the success of the team. The best teams are made up of an equal balance of all four, so think about the personality styles when hiring for open positions and when scheduling shifts.

The following is a breakdown of the positive traits of each style. Later we'll talk about what goes wrong when the personality is carried to an extreme. As you review the characteristics, think about the personalities that make up your staff. Which of these descriptions describes each employee? Which best describes you?

The contributor: This personality is very task-oriented, technically adept and instrumental in pushing the rest of the team to set high performance standards. You can count on the contributor to complete all the tasks in his or her regular job area as well as other tasks for the team. He or she has a clear sense of priorities and will always accept responsibility for his or her actions. A born trainer, contributors are at their best when sharing better ways of doing things with others. Contributors are great leaders in the kitchen, or detail-oriented bus staff who are highly dependable.

The collaborator: This personality is very goal-oriented. He or she is quick to pitch in and help out others on the floor when they need it, so look for collaborator qualities in all your front-of-the-house staff. The collaborator is quick to remind the team of its goals and help the team see how its

> "Know your people, know their strengths. Know your work and its requirements. Bring them into closer alignment. It seems terribly obvious."
>
> — *Ned Herrmann, founder of the Ned Herrmann Group and former head of management training for General Electric Co.*

work fits into the big picture. He or she works harder than anyone to achieve team goals, even working outside of defined roles to help the team. The collaborator is no superstar – he or she is happy to share the limelight.

The communicator: This process-oriented personality is an effective listener and facilitator of involvement and conflict resolution. An open communication style makes him or her a great floor manager, server or greeter. The communicator is also a good trainer because of an ability to provide descriptive, specific feedback. And this type's attentive listening skills will help the team resolve problems. The communicator's enthusiasm is effective in getting people involved while helping them to relax, get to know each other and have fun by joking, laughing and discussing personal interests.

The challenger: Sometimes a little more difficult to deal with, the challenger exhibits candor and openness which helps the team explore better ways of doing things. If the person can be candid without being nasty, this is a personality you'll want on all your teams to help trouble-shoot problems. He or she is willing to disagree openly with leadership, raise questions about goals and blow the whistle on illegal or unethical activities. Not one to back down easily, he or she will speak out even when views are contrary to those of the team majority. Highly principled, the challenger pushes the team to set high ethical standards and achieve team goals by taking well-conceived risks.

Name, Rank and Serial Number

Don't think of team-player styles as a secretive employee rating system. Their purpose is to help you build well-balanced teams whose members recognize their own personality traits and know how to accentuate positive behaviors. During a staff meeting, describe the four styles – both positive and negative traits. Let your employees think about which style best describes them. It will help them accept a more active role on the team because they can see how their unique personality rounds out the group.

10 Bad Seeds

Ineffective team-player personalities

Too much of a good thing is never good for the team. In the last section we listed the positive traits of the four different team-player styles. But each has its negative side, as well. When a team player's negative traits take over, he or she becomes an ineffective member of the team, resulting in wasted time and effort, lost opportunities, poor customer relations, low morale, high turnover and, ultimately, a negative impact on your bottom line. Here's what ineffective team-players look like:

The ineffective contributor: The task-oriented contributor, who usually helps the team by providing useful technical information and by being a model of excellence, can become ineffective by pushing for unrealistic performance standards, losing sight of the big picture or having a lack of patience with the need for a positive team climate. Perfectionistic attitudes on efficiency, following rules and minimizing risk make this person too short-sighted to benefit the team.

The ineffective collaborator: The goal-directed collaborator who pushes the team to "stay the course" and achieve its goals becomes ineffective when he or she fails to challenge those goals when necessary. This personality tends to do a great job at being "visionary" but sometimes has little patience for the work involved to achieve the vision. He or she may lack attention to the basic team tasks and work-area performance, and fail to focus on meeting the needs of other team players.

The ineffective communicator: The process-oriented communicator can become ineffective by failing to challenge or confront other team members, by not recognizing the equal importance of completing tasks and making progress toward team goals, or by overusing humor. When the team doesn't succeed, the ineffective communicator assumes the reason must be that the team doesn't work well together and proceeds to push for increased emphasis on listening, feedback and participation, when the real problem is in task completion.

The ineffective challenger: The challenger can become ineffective by not knowing when to back off and let the team move on, by pushing the team to take risks that are beyond reason, by becoming self-righteous, rigid and inflexible or by using so-called honesty as a cover for attacks on other members. These are people who love a fight. They enjoy getting a shot in at the boss, pushing the rules to the limit or daring you to knock that chip off their shoulder. Although the team needs people who will speak out about important issues, it does not need people who simply enjoy being disagreeable.

TIP

Behave Yourselves

Here are a few ways to help problem players improve their behavior:

Let the team solve its own problems. **At team training meetings, lead a group discussion on acceptable behaviors – completing tasks, participating in discussions, confrontations with other members, etc. Don't single anyone out, but give them an opportunity to give each other feedback on their performance. *Meet privately* and ask the problem person: "Why are you on this team?" What is your role? Do you have concerns about the way the team works together?" Uncover the causes of resistance. He or she may have a personal crisis that's spilling over into work. *Listen.* Maybe the person has a point. Sometimes what you perceive as ineffective team play is simply your inability to understand and appreciate a person with another style.**

Cut Your Losses

Terminating employees who refuse to join the team

Team-building requires a commitment from everyone on your staff. But often you'll find a few who simply refuse to participate. Recognize that their negativity is contagious. As it spreads throughout your staff, morale drops lower and lower. And with it plunges your staff's productivity. That's no way to build a team.

Your only recourse is to get rid of low-performing employees. Weed out the trouble-makers, the loafers and the whiners to make room for more positive employees.

It's a harsh step – and you may ask if you can really *afford* to do something so drastic. Truth is, though, you really can't afford *not* to. Make no mistake about it: Your team-building efforts will fail if you can't get employee buy-in. That means *all* your employees.

But, before you go cleaning house, understand that an employee's refusal to join the team is usually an indication of a deeper problem.

Ask yourself what it is about a particular employee that's not working out. Attitude? Bad habits? Ability to do the work? Relations with other staffers?

Then ask yourself if there's something that can be done to correct the problems and avoid an emotional termination. Could that employee have been better trained? Confusion is the result of ineffective or nonexistent training. And confused people cannot act.

> **"If you can't change your people, then you *must* change your people."**
> — *Tom Hopkins,*
> *author, speaker*

Plus, better work habits will earn the employee more respect from his or her co-workers. Maintain an open dialogue with employees who are having trouble. Begin the process informally, giving employees the opportunity to be trained and change their attitude and behavior before pulling out the pink slips.

When you meet with them, be clear and specific about the problems and about what changes you expect. And be sure to follow up later. Applaud their improvements – it shows they're trying and worthy of recognition.

TIP

Moving On

Studies have shown that 80 percent of Americans have been fired at one time or another. When it becomes clear that firing an employee is the only possible recourse, you owe it to that employee to act decisively. Firings are difficult, but not fatal. Here are a few tips to get you through termination meetings quickly and painlessly:

Be as considerate as you can – think of how you would want to be treated. Make the meeting as brief as possible. Focus on specific behaviors and actions – not personalities. Be sure to follow the necessary legal guidelines for firing, including reference to previous written warnings, non-performance according to job requirements, etc. Do not review old sources of dispute – it will just cause a fight. Make it clear to the employee that it's too late for another chance.

12 Climate Control

Improving morale

> "If you hire talented people and treat them badly, they'll screw things up for you. They'll slow you down and be rude to customers. Talented people don't necessarily do better unless you manage them well."
>
> — *Donald Clifton, Chairman, The Gallup Organization*

A negative work environment will destroy your team-building efforts. Before you can get employees to work together, you have to make them happy about working for you. How do you do that? Be a leader, not a boss.

Do you thank them for their dedication, praise them for accomplishments and have tolerance for honest mistakes? If you treat your employees with hostility and indifference, how will they treat each other? Worse – how will they treat your customers?

People want to succeed. Nobody comes to work to fail. It seems obvious – so why do so many managers operate on the principle that if people aren't watched and supervised, they'll bungle the job? Once you have the right people trained and in position with your team strategies laid out, you shouldn't have to worry about them getting the job done. Trust them to do their job just as you are trusted to do yours.

Be consistent on policies, procedures, training and communication. Employees want to be dealt with equally. Showing favor to only part of the staff will create resentment throughout. Be fair when it comes to scheduling and discipline. Don't bend the rules for anyone no matter what the circumstances – and don't just leave discipline to the whim of a supervisor.

Try to teach everyone on staff something new every day. It will keep their jobs from becoming mundane.

Stop work-related gossip *before* it starts. Communicate with your people about everything that affects their working environment. Announce staff changes – hirings, firings, promotions. The decisions you make behind closed doors will inevitably leak out. Count on it.

When you have to fire an employee or someone quits, call a meeting. Announce why – honestly. Conversely, when an employee's great performance warrants a salary increase, announce that, too. It's an occasion for celebration, not a decision that should be hidden for fear of staff jealousy. Plus, it keeps that pie in the sky for those striving for better.

Lay out concepts and ideas, but let your people execute them. Step back and allow them to *own* their work. Communicate your vision of an ideal restaurant to your staff. Be sure everyone understands it.

Above all, truly appreciate your employees. They can make you or break you.

Take It to the Board

Form an "Employee Board" of five or six employees from all departments in the restaurant. Assign as their first task assessing employee satisfaction. Are they happy with their jobs? Do they know how they fit into the organization in terms of its goals and objectives? The group should be headed by an executive officer and no direct supervisors should be present so the employees can speak freely. The Employee Board will also be a great means for gathering facts from employees regarding problem areas in the restaurant, or concerns they have with their work environment. Utilize an agenda so the board meetings are constructive – not just gripe sessions. Give the Board fun tasks, as well, like testing new menu items, planning staff parties, etc.

13 Prove It

Proving benefits of teamwork to staff

> **"A coach is someone who makes you do what you don't want to do so you can be who you always wanted to be."**
> — *Tom Landry*

You obviously can't do it without them. That's why you have to convince your employees that teamwork benefits *them*. The first task in building a team is to get all the players on the same page. Call a staff meeting. Read them the first four sections of this book, defining teamwork, what it looks like when it fails and when it's working well.

Then use examples from your own operation. Point out what types of things go wrong on a typical shift and outline what types of situations you'd like to see. You'll probably hear a few giggles when you describe an ideal shift at your restaurant. But follow up by tuning in to everyone's favorite radio station WII-FM – "What's In It For Me" to become a team player?

There's a lot in it for them, actually. Describe the impact good teamwork has on customer service. More customers means a better business – more tips for servers, raises for the kitchen crew. Money talks! And, with a more collaborative atmosphere, they'll have more fun at work every day.

Some employees will still resist because, to them, more customers means more work. That's where the big leap of faith comes in. You have to convince them that, with help from everyone on the staff, there *won't* be an uncomfortable amount of extra work.

Ask for their help in identifying specific team-oriented behaviors that, individually, amount to nothing earth shattering, but, together, make all the difference in the world. Go around the room asking for input on what constitutes teamwork and what does it look like when it's working well. Encourage them to be honest. A buser might say, "It takes just as much time for servers to find me and yell at me about empty water glasses as it does for them to grab a pitcher and fill the glasses."

Help them to find solutions, using statements that begin with, "I appreciate it when ..." A bartender might say, "I appreciate it when servers dump dirty glasses before they give them to me to wash." Write all their responses on a flip chart.

Then outline your "Action Plan" for creating a team environment. Describe for your staff changes you'll make in policies that will foster a team atmosphere – hiring, salary reviews, bonuses, incentives. Pass out new employee handbooks that detail those policies. Establish your expectations: participation in daily pre-shift meetings and monthly team training meetings, leading shifts and generally being open to new ways of doing things.

Finish up by outlining your team mission statements and goals – goals you can't achieve without everyone's help. Show them how achieving those goals benefits them just as much as they benefit the operation.

I'm No Joiner

Before you can get employee buy-in to your team-building efforts, try to understand why many resist the idea. Here are three common reasons. *Lack of conviction:* Despite studies to the contrary, many people don't believe teams really outperform individuals. They may believe that teams waste time in unproductive meetings, or that while teams help people get along better, they hinder individual productivity. *Personal discomfort and risk:* Some people believe team membership is a personal burden. They worry about their ability to get along, speak up or depend on others. *Weak organizational-performance ethics:* Without a commitment from managers, employees feel insecure about dedicating themselves to the work at hand. To instill a feeling of confidence, managers must send a clear message that everyone's performance on the team really matters to the restaurant's success.

14 Change Is Good

Overcoming a resistance to change

> **"He was a bold man that first ate an oyster."**
> — *Jonathan Swift*

When teams begin to form, work roles *will* change. So begin preparing for the inevitable resistance. It will start with the familiar complaint: "That's not my job," or an assortment of variations: "We've never done it that way before," and "Do I get a pay increase for doing that?"

Many of the problems that teams suffer generally fall under the category "resistance to change."

No matter how hard managers push employees toward constantly improved performance, there will always be those employees who prefer stable, predictable work – jobs that can be explained on a half-page job description and mastered in a half-day training session. After all, it's just restaurant work ... right?

In a team environment, employees will often be asked to learn several jobs, be ready to switch jobs, move into leadership positions, master new skills and back up others. It's no wonder you'll find resistance.

Nowhere is this resistance stronger than among supervisors and managers. For many, not only will their job duties change, but they will be asked to change their communication style, the way they give instructions and how they use their power. "Position power," based on title, gives way to personal power. And when you ask people to give that up and help out the lower-level employees, expect that a few feathers will be ruffled.

When you make the decision to change your culture, no one will be exempt from the pain of that change. But don't let that scare you. Instead, think about how best to introduce the change – gradual change is often best.

And think of how you will deal with those who are hurt by the change. It's often easiest if everyone on staff is asked to make changes. There shouldn't be any exemptions – particularly among management staff. If egos become bruised, treat the injured parties with respect and care. Leaders and supervisors who lose their authority and whose concerns are ignored can poison the rest of the team with their grievances.

TIP

Be Reasonable

To make change less painful for everyone:

- **Make sure that what you are asking for is reasonable.**

- **Involve team members in planning and executing the change. Ask for their input and work with them on putting the new order in place.**

- **Make sure there are sound business reasons for any change you make, and communicate those reasons to team members. It's surprising how much more understanding they can be when they see the big picture.**

"The will to win
is not as
important as
the will to
prepare to win."
— *Bobby Knight*

CHAPTER TWO:
Play by Play

Pro sports teams make executing the plays look so spontaneous. What armchair quarterbacks tend to forget is that most of the moves the players make are carefully choreographed on paper or a chalkboard and memorized by every member of the team.

As coach of your restaurant teams, you should develop a few strategic plays of your own. Forget spontaneity. By mapping out a plan for all your players to follow, you can guarantee that everyone will be in position to serve your guests' needs.

On the upcoming pages, we'll detail the nuts and bolts of working together in a team environment – how to put abstract management theories to work in the hustle and bustle of the typical restaurant. We'll discuss how to schedule shifts for the best team performance and how teams can prepare "in the huddle" before each shift. We'll also take a look at typical restaurant positions to see how each employee's role helps the team succeed. And we'll discuss how special teams can benefit your operation.

Games People Play

Types of restaurant teams

Corporate America's traditional teaming concept takes on a whole new dimension in a restaurant environment. Your employees don't sit around in meetings all day, discussing projects and shuffling papers. Your *customers* are your project. And the mission of each team is to serve those customers well. But each team will need to go about it in different ways.

There are two types of restaurant teams: front-line and production. Each sports its own structure, with varying behaviors required of its employees, and different strengths, vulnerabilities, limitations and requirements.

Your production – or kitchen – team's mission is to efficiently produce the best quality product at the lowest cost. And in most restaurants, every member has a different point in the production line.

Think of your kitchen team in terms of baseball: The players are all on the same team, but they each play a different position. While players may occasionally need to back each other up in the field, the second baseman never throws a pitch. And when one player drops the ball, it affects every player on the team.

Your front-of-the-house team is more like a hockey team. They each have a primary – rather than "fixed" – position. To serve customers most effectively, front-of-the-house team members must complete their own tasks *and* cover for their teammates whenever necessary, adjusting to their team-

> **"I knew we were in for a long season when we lined up for the national anthem on opening day and one of my players said, 'Every time I hear that song I have a bad game.'"**
>
> — Jim Leyland,
> Baseball Manager

mates' strengths and weaknesses. They must continually adjust to the changing demands of the game while together pressing toward the goal – and to win, they must work together to keep mistakes from getting through.

It's important for you to know the difference between the two types of restaurant teams. It will affect every team decision you make – incentives, rewards, scheduling, choosing leaders. And it's equally important to let your employees know what game they're playing. That's why you'll need to define the difference for them as you begin to build your team culture.

Social Hour

Building teams is easier if your people know each other on a personal level. But friendship and camaraderie don't happen by themselves. You can help the process by throwing a staff party where employees can socialize. Create a "Staff Yearbook" form. Ask personal questions about their favorite music, the last movie they've seen, their dream job, names of their pets, their "ideal" weekend. While crew mingle, have each fill out a form. Take Polaroid pictures of everyone and attach them to the questionnaires. Hang the pages around the restaurant for staff to read. Later, compile the forms and Polaroids into a "yearbook" binder. As you hire new people, show them the yearbook to help them get acquainted with co-workers – and have them fill out their own questionnaire during their training.

16 Great Expectations

Establishing roles within teams

Tired of hearing the excuses yet? "Sorry, that's not in my job description." "Sorry, not my section." "Sorry, I'm on my break." Nothing destroys team-building efforts more than excuses for not helping each other out. But often you'll find that employees *are* willing to do their part for the team – they just don't want to be taken advantage of by their co-workers.

Part of the problem can be job descriptions that are too task-oriented. Managers have spent years constricting their employees with bullet-pointed duties listed on a piece of paper. Once employees complete the tasks on the list, they clock out and go home. The narrow confines of a task-oriented job description leave far too many gray areas.

An employee's "role" on the team goes beyond his or her job description. Sure, you need to outline specific tasks, but also outline your expectations.

For instance, you may want busers to load bus tubs, clean the premises and fill water glasses in their sections. But you also *expect* them to complete the work safely, minimize breakage, back up other busers when their sections get busy and help servers do anything it takes to fulfill the needs of guests.

That's their role on the team, and it's tough to understand when it's defined with a bullet-pointed list. That's why you should talk about it.

"Gray areas" are the usual cause of conflicts among staffers. They often surface as "personality differences," when the problem is really rooted in a poor understanding of each other's role.

Effective teamwork involves task *interdependence*. To help clarify that concept along with team member roles, revise your job descriptions to include role expectations. Make sure that tasks are evenly distributed throughout the team so no member is overly burdened.

Call a team meeting. Pass out the descriptions and go through them point by point with the group. Have *the team* outline the gray areas. Let them further define the roles so they'll all understand what's expected of them by other team members.

Sample Job Description: Server

The server is an important part of the front-of-the-house team. His or her role is to anticipate guests' needs, providing timely, friendly, efficient service. Tasks servers are expected to perform include greeting guests; taking food/drink orders; garnishing and serving food/drinks; carrying trays of food/drinks; ensuring food/drink items meet guests' satisfaction; removing dishes/glasses, trash, capping ashtrays and refilling beverages; entering orders on a POS register; preparing, presenting and receiving payment for guests' checks; loading bus tubs and unloading at dishwasher station; sanitizing tables and chairs; resetting tables; restocking service stations; maintaining common area; sweeping/mopping floor. Servers are expected to complete the listed tasks within their assigned section, and help out other sections whenever possible.

17 Leading the Way

Choosing your team leaders

Teams tend to have leaders and leaders tend to create teams. A leader is the glue that holds the team together, ever pushing members toward a common goal. Your teams won't succeed without them. But in a restaurant environment where daily shift changes mean constantly changing team membership, effective leadership becomes a challenge.

Choose several likely candidates in each department, looking for strong leadership qualities, a take-charge attitude and an ability to present information in front of a group. Train them in any areas needing improvement. Their role on the team will be two-fold: In a team-building capacity, they will lead pre-shift team meetings, skills training sessions, discussions on goal-setting, problem-solving and role definitions. In a team-member capacity, they will set the tone for the shift, maintaining communication between team members and providing constant feedback.

After leaders complete their training, you should schedule carefully to ensure that one trained leader will be present at every shift in every department. And when you announce your team-building strategies to your staff, introduce the team leaders, describing what their roles will be and why you selected them for the added responsibilities.

When choosing leader candidates, you're not necessarily looking for the best servers or the top cooks – and don't simply hand out the title to assistant managers and kitchen managers. Team leadership is a job for people who inspire other members to succeed – and who carry a full share of the load themselves. Pick the natural team-players – those who've always been quick to help out others. Over time, select and train additional team leaders to take over if someone else should leave, or just to provide teams with some variety.

Many operators make the mistake of giving leaders a great deal of authority and too much responsibility for the success of the team. It's easier for people to have someone tell them what to do, when to do it and how to do it. And it's convenient to have someone else to blame. But over the long haul, a team will not be successful if the leader carries the burden for ensuring that the team reaches its goals.

In successful teams, leadership tasks and qualities are shared among team members. If the team fails, everybody fails. While the formal leader has certain administrative responsibilities like leading training meetings, etc., it's within the leader's authority to solicit the help of other team members from time to time to serve as trainers, communicators and problem solvers.

TIP

The Role of the Team Leader

- **Asking team members about problems in processes to help them think about solutions.**
- **Training individual team members in both task and team-building skills.**
- **Facilitating team interactions by encouraging balanced participation, summarizing differences and agreements and brainstorming alternative actions.**
- **Defining team member roles, and making sure members are assuming them.**
- **Managing team boundaries.**
- **Coordinating team activities by communicating with other teams and monitoring performances.**
- **Providing formal and informal recognition.**

18 Getting Started

Stages of team development

Leading a team is not the same as leading individuals. Rather than match leadership styles to ability and motivation, you have to adapt them to stages of team development.

When you begin training your team leaders, be sure they understand the four predictable stages through which most teams progress:

Stage 1: Forming
Here team members are guarded and more interested in completing just their own individual tasks. They wait for the leader to tell them ways to help out others. At this stage, leaders must continually remind members of the team's mission and purpose, and make them all feel welcome by describing how each member fits into the big picture.

Stage 2: Focusing
This stage begins with questions. While it can be an uncomfortable stage, it is necessary for helping the team members buy into the mission. It's here that friction shows itself and power struggles may erupt. In effect, the group is testing the boundaries leaders laid out in Stage 1.

Stage 3: Performing
Here's where people are productive and share responsibility and a sense of purpose. People trust each other. At this stage, leaders should offer support, recognize people's efforts, listen well and steer communication in productive ways.

Stage 4: Leveling

The group makes great strides in Stage 3, which gives it a sense of satisfaction and, eventually, complacency. To offset this tendency, leaders should take time to celebrate successes and build in times for refocusing the group. If the group has leveled, leaders can try refocusing it with problem solving. If that doesn't work, they should go back to Stage 1 for a refresher.

Back to the Drawing Board

Here are some of the factors that can send a developing team back to Stage One:

- **Team members quitting**
- **A loss of trust**
- **Losing sight of the goal**
- **Poor communication**

- **Low morale**
- **Terminations**
- **New leadership**
- **Poorly defined roles**

19 In the Huddle

Conducting effective pre-shift team meetings

Just like the football team which huddles up before each play, your restaurant teams need a chance to get together every day to prepare for the coming shift. Daily pre-shift team meetings are the anchor for creating a team environment in your operation. Here are some tips on managing them effectively:

Keep the meetings short and sweet, five or 10 minutes per day and always start and end on time.

Use this time to designate each team player's role for the day. Conduct a group discussion on yesterday's successes and challenges. What worked well? Where did the breakdowns occur? Ask for team players' input on how to avoid those problems today.

Think dialogue, not monologue. Shift leaders should speak 20 percent of the time and seek feedback during the other 80 percent. Involve everyone in the training: Each day, have one team member present a brief training session on techniques that have worked well for him or her. For example, instead of telling servers how to increase appetizer sales, call on servers to help their teammates by describing the techniques that have helped them make the sale.

Encourage feedback. Have each staffer demonstrate how he or she is going to apply the principles that the team has discussed. Conduct brief role-playing scenarios during which staffers can work together to practice their new techniques.

Have team leaders verbally quiz their teammates on product knowledge, daily specials and upcoming events or promotions.

Don't leave out the kitchen crew! Have a brief team meeting every day, during which leaders discuss challenges and conduct training sessions on cost control, speeding up ticket times and ensuring quality.

Set the day's team goals and incentives, and distribute yesterday's team awards. And conclude every session with a little open communication time during which team members can discuss any topic – whether it be a constructive gripe session or a chance to pat each other on the back.

Shift Into Gear

Tips for holding effective pre-shift team meetings:

- **Keep it short – five or 10 minutes per day.**

- **Think dialogue. Have team leaders verbally quiz employees on product knowledge, daily specials and upcoming events or promotions.**

- **Conduct brief role-playing scenarios during which staff can practice their new techniques.**

- **Set daily sales goals and introduce incentives for servers and bartenders.**

- **Encourage employees to practice the new skills in the next shift – and follow up out on the floor.**

20) Put Me In, Coach

Scheduling informal "shift" teams

Putting the right players into the right positions can ensure the team functions at its highest level. But that can be a challenge when you're dealing with shift workers. Most industries' teams have fixed memberships with the same players working together on the same shift every day. That's why most operators don't believe teams can work together effectively in restaurants.

Truth is, though, your teams *can* function well with an ever-changing membership. In fact, the informality and changing dynamics of the group's makeup can help workers perform even better. When members have the opportunity to continually work with new people, they learn different approaches, different techniques – some they may want to copy.

But you will want to set some guidelines for team membership, and schedule effectively to maximize the performance of the team during every shift.

Look back to the different team-player personality styles in idea number 9. And remember that teams function most effectively when there's a balance of those styles on every shift.

Be sure to schedule a trained leader on every shift. It's his or her responsibility to pull the players together for pre-shift team meetings, teach them something new, set shift roles, goals and incentives. It's during this time that team players will mingle, socialize and build the rapport that will be essential for working together effectively.

When possible, try to keep at least some of the players constant on every shift. That shouldn't be too hard since many of your employees prefer and request standardized work hours.

You can save yourself time and reduce complaints by passing the scheduling responsibilities on to the team itself. Tell members that every week, members of each shift team are required to fill a certain number of shifts together. For example, Team "A" must fill three lunch shifts and four dinner shifts this week. The teams usually get together on their own time for about half an hour to decide what days they want to work, what days they want off. It's a great team-building exercise that teaches members how to collaborate.

Scheduling for Success

You can build teamwork by being accommodating in scheduling whenever you can. Here are some tips for smart scheduling that helps prevent burnout:

- **Give two days off in a row.**
- **Strive for five-day work weeks.**
- **Don't ask employees to close one day and open the next.**
- **Create a small overlap between shifts to ease transition for both shifts.**
- **Invest in training – schedule an experienced employee to accompany a new employee throughout the entire shift.**

21 In the Trenches

Your front-of-the-house team

One of your challenges in establishing a team culture in the front of the house will be to change mindsets. If servers are used to being singled out as selling superstars and tipped on their individual performance, why would they want to help other servers with their sections? And when they're encouraged to sell, sell, sell, there's little motivation to handle all the extra little things that keep guests coming back.

The truth is that problems in section four will eventually affect section three. And the more front-of-the-house workers can back each other up on the floor, the less problems all of them will encounter. When one server gets thrown into the weeds, it creates delays in the kitchen which will affect other servers' sections.

The same is true of bartenders. If they get behind, everyone's section suffers. If the greeter gets swamped, servers don't get a regular flow of guests. And if a buser gets behind, customer needs are left unmet. If guests receive poor service because any employee is too rushed to do his or her job, they probably won't come back. That affects everyone.

Every member of the team has his or her individual tasks, which usually come first. But there are other tasks that sometimes get left undone when things get hectic – pre-busing tables, keeping the place clean, preparing silverware rollups, running a bus tub back to the kitchen, answering phones, seating guests when the greeter's away or simply stopping by another server's tables to check on guests.

After you define every player's primary tasks, then define secondary tasks to complete, as needed, in other sections and in other positions. The secondary tasks become a window of opportunity to help out others. And the overlapping responsibilities will ensure that everything gets done.

On the pages that follow, we'll outline these "windows of opportunity" for each of your front-line team members.

Reversing Roles

Here's how your employees, by position, can help out others when they have a few minutes to spare:

Servers: **Watch guests in other sections, fulfill any guests' needs; run food orders out for other servers; pre-bus tables; run bus tubs to the back; greet and seat guests; answer ringing phones.**

Greeters: **Communicate with other members of the team; pre-bus tables; run bus tubs to the back; run food orders out; help servers sell.**

Busers: **Fulfill guests' needs in their own section and an adjacent section; learn selling skills; run food orders out; answer ringing phones; cross-train in back-bartender's duties.**

Bartenders: **Run drinks out to guests; open wine bottles for servers; answer ringing phones.**

22 The Buddy System

The server's role on the team

Form a "Buddy System" that encourages servers to be aware of not only their guests, but the guests in an adjacent section. Draw your restaurant's floor plan on a white board and use a grease pencil to "buddy up" server stations. Assign servers different primary and secondary stations from one day to the next.

A server's buddy becomes the person to call on for a little extra help. Buddies are responsible for helping with pre-busing each other's tables, running food orders, running credit cards and taking orders for each other. The buddy's role is simply to keep an eye peeled. Does a guest need a refill? A clean fork? Some more cream?

Communication is the key. Have your servers come up with a non-verbal signal that indicates they have a spare minute to help out their buddies – an "OK" sign, for example. They can also develop a series of hand signals for tasks that need to be completed. A server in the weeds can signal to his or her buddy that table four's orders are ready – could he or she run them out?

Also create code words to indicate what stage of the meal guests are at. If a server can't get to one of his or her tables, what a help it is for a buddy to come to the rescue. For example, if servers know what to do at the "initial greeting" stage of a guest's meal, a buddy can come in to say: "Hi, folks, welcome to our restaurant. Pam's going to be serving you tonight, but before she gets here to take your orders, I thought I'd stop by to tell you about our great drink specials ..."

Since buddy teams rotate every day, they improve teamwork and create a more friendly atmosphere. You never know who'll be your next buddy! To keep sales flowing, set up contests in which buddy teams compete for high sales of items such as large beers, appetizers or desserts. The buddy team that sells the most of a designated item within one week wins the prize.

Seat Yourself

There are plenty more front-of-the-house functions a server can handle to support his or her teammates:

- **Cross-train servers to do the greeter's job so they can help out in a pinch.**

- **Teach them to never pass by a waiting guest without a smile and a greeting: "Hi, folks. Someone will be right with you." Or better yet, encourage servers to seat guests themselves. Servers who complain about not making enough tips because of empty sections will jump at the chance to fill their own seats.**

- **Teach servers never to pass by a ringing phone. And while you're at it, work on their phone-service skills.**

23 Please Be Seated

The greeter's role on the team

It all starts at the front door. And when things start to heat up, the greeters always feel it first. The greeter is the person with the most valuable view of the restaurant. From their stand in the front, greeters can see how busy things are in each section and control how busy things become for everyone. And since they're constantly on their feet, moving through the restaurant, they have a great opportunity to help out others.

One of the greeter's most important functions is team communicator. Often when a rush starts, employees don't know it until it's too late. A greeter can help by spreading guests thinly through the sections and letting everyone know that things are heating up. After seating a rush of guests, he or she should take a run back to the kitchen to warn the team to get prepared. He or she should stop by the bar, as well, to make sure they're ready.

Teach greeters the "full hands in, full hands out" philosophy that's typically reserved for bus staff. Any time they head back to the kitchen, they should take a route through the dining area, looking for dishes to be cleared or debris to be picked up. And in the back, they should check for orders that can be run out to guests.

The greeter can also help out servers by making menu recommendations to guests as they're seated. For example, if the servers' goal for the shift is increased appetizer sales, a greeter can tailor sales dialogue accordingly: "Julie's going to be serving you tonight. But before she gets here to tell you about our menu, you might want to think about tonight's appetizer special. It's our ultimate nacho platter and it goes great with our house margaritas. Have a great meal!"

Ensure that all your front-line workers follow the same game plan by attaching a laminated floor plan to a clipboard to be kept at the greeter stand. Have staff mark it up with a grease pencil to indicate any changes that occur in a station during the shift. The floor plan will help if greeters don't know servers' names, if tables have been rearranged or if servers are unfamiliar with their stations. The clipboard is also "greener" than making excessive photocopies. Keep a digital watch attached to a clipboard for the door staff to use just in case any of them arrive at work without a watch.

Name Dropping

A nice touch guests will appreciate is for host staff to help servers learn and use guests' names. Have greeters write the names of incoming guests and their respective table numbers on a slip of paper – possibly even on the guest check – and hand it to the appropriate server. Later, when servers greet the table, they can address guests by name. Hold a weekly contest to see which servers can remember the most names. Don't forget to reward the greeters, too. Hold a server vote to see who on the host staff is best at "name dropping." Reward contest winners with gifts such as address books, gift certificates or a dinner for two at your operation.

24 Catch the Bus

The buser's role on the team

> "I have a simple philosophy. Fill what's empty. Empty what's full. Scratch where it itches."
>
> — *Alice Roosevelt Longworth*

Think of your busers as servers-in-training. In a team-oriented environment, they still clear the tables and fill the water glasses, backing up the buser in an adjacent section. But they also can play a key role in meeting guests' needs.

Busers, who field all kinds of customer questions, should go through server sales training to learn ways to maximize any contact they have with guests.

For example, which response would you prefer your buser use? The guest says, "Could you find our server? We've changed our mind about ordering desserts." 1. "Uh. Yeah, inna minute." Or 2. "Sure. Do you know what you might like? I just passed through the kitchen and saw Curtis dishing out a strawberry pie that looked incredible. Or, if you're in the mood for a chocolate fix, my favorite's the Brownie Sundae. Shall I ask Pam to bring you either of those?"

Motivate busers to help servers sell by offering prizes to the pair that sells the most of a particular menu item.

Cross-train busers in back-bar service. When a slow shift suddenly turns busy, there's often no one else on staff to help the bartender set up kegs, bring in cases of beer and wash glasses. Train busers to veer off their normal dining-room route from time to time to check on things at the bar.

More flexible than the barkeep, a buser can chase down, say, more fruit garnishes from the kitchen, allowing the bar staff to stay with guests. The simple act of teamwork can have a big impact on the quality of service. Busers can help make the dishwasher's job a little easier, too, simply by scraping food and waste off plates and sorting silverware.

Raise the Flag

Busers can help out greeters, as well. When greeters see an empty table from across the room, they may assume it's ready for new guests. It's not necessarily so. Often guests are seated at a table that's decorated with a coffee spill, a couple of old cold fries and a tip for the server. Eliminate this customer turnoff by having busers and other staff "flag the table." When busers can't get to a table right away, or they've cleared it but haven't yet wiped it down, they should stick a ketchup bottle at the end of the table so the greeter knows not to seat the table at that moment. If your operation doesn't keep bottled ketchup on the table, designate another "flag," such as a table tent or flower vase. Flagging tables gives host staff the vital information necessary for peak performance. It's also a handy visual reminder for the employee responsible for clearing the table.

25 Taking the Heat

Your kitchen team

Minimize waste. Prevent accidents. Control costs. Produce the best quality product. Oh, and make it quick. No wonder the atmosphere in the kitchen feels like a pressure cooker. But your kitchen employees can take the heat – or can they?

The kitchen sees the most turnover industry-wide. The root of the problem lies in the long-held perception that kitchen positions are secondary to front-of-the-house positions, and that kitchen crew members are somehow less skilled and more easily replaced. Any manager who values his cooks will certainly challenge that opinion. That's why it's beneficial to remind kitchen workers of their importance in the big picture.

Their team's contributions often seem to go unsung because, from their view in the back, they rarely see the end user of their product. Remind them that good service isn't just the front-of-the-house team's responsibility. It takes a concerted effort from everyone on the kitchen crew, too. The prep cook, the food expediter and the cook are just as important in providing a great dining experience for guests.

Serving those guests well means a kitchen production line that operates at its most efficient level. The kitchen team's goals are achieved only when each worker in the production chain performs at his or her peak.

That's why it's individual accountability that matters most in the kitchen. Intensive skills training is the foundation for team development, because if any member of the team can't handle his or her own tasks, mistakes and delays negatively affect everyone else on the line. When one team member gets dragged down by another's mistakes, resentment builds, as does the urge to drag the next team member down, too. Encourage the teammates to solve the problem, not perpetuate it.

And while they shouldn't have to constantly "back each other up" when things get hectic like members of the front-line team, kitchen employees should have the ability to communicate with each other to get the job done. So train them in the proper communication techniques they'll need to help each other out.

Also, cross-train members of your kitchen crew. They'll not only be able to back each other up when necessary, but keep their jobs from becoming mundane. And, should your cook come down with the flu, you won't be wiped out for the shift since you'll be able to rotate your prep cook in to cover the orders.

Hail to the Chef

Just like in the front-of-the-house, when you conceive incentives for waste watching, speed or quality control for kitchen crew members, be sure awards are based on the team's effort, not the individual's. Offer your kitchen staff a bonus based on the amount of money saved on food cost versus the budget each month. Run a contest offering a dime for every properly prepared ticket finished in 15 minutes or less. At the end of the shift, split the money among all the team members on the line.

26 Dishing It Out

The dishwasher's role on the team

> "The smallest hole will eventually empty the largest container in a restaurant, unless it was made intentionally for drainage, in which case it will clog."
>
> — *Tito Mendez, Kitchen Manager*

It's a dirty job, but your dishwashers are back there doing it for the benefit of the rest of the staff. And you know how bad things can get when they can't get their job done – mistakes get made, breakage occurs, accidents happen and, eventually, every department in the operation suffers.

The dishwasher's limited view of the restaurant prevents him or her from directly contributing to either the production or the front-line teams.

But their role is still essential to achieving the operation's goals. How could a restaurant operation possibly succeed without clean dishes to serve its delectable meals on?

Here are some ways both front-of-the-house and kitchen teams can help out the dishwasher:

- If a glass or plate gets broken, employees should ask the dishwasher where he or she would prefer the pieces be placed. Sharp, broken objects lurking under the suds cause an undue amount of accidents.

- If your employees have time, they should knock some of the food on the plate into the refuse receptacle in the dish area. It helps the dishwasher get the job done quicker – especially when it's busy.

- Busers should set plates into the bus tub or onto the dish table. Never use the "short toss" method. There will be less breakage, less noise and fewer stitches.

- Separate the silverware. If everyone took the time to do this, there wouldn't be such a long wait for fresh silverware.

- Everyone likes to clock out and go home at a decent hour. But closing time is the point on every shift that dishwashers feel the most distance from the rest of the staff. Make them feel a part of the team by designating a buser or kitchen team member to help out once they've finished their own closing responsibilities.

Trash Your Losses

Dishwashers play an important role in your efforts to control operational costs. When they or careless busers and servers throw away expensive flatware or dishes, that's money down the drain. You've made it part of your kitchen crew's mission to be active waste watchers. Illustrate the importance of waste watching to your dish staff, as well. Give them a goal by offering an incentive: At the end of each shift, have the dishwasher slowly dump the contents of one trash can into an empty one, searching for tossed items. Reward a dollar for each item recovered. Also, nail an empty five-quart bucket to the wall by the dishwasher in which to throw dry, uncontaminated sugar, cracker, salt and pepper packets that were left on clean plates. Have the dishwasher reconcile the bucket's contents back to their proper storage places. Reward the effort with a cash bonus or gift certificate for each full bucket reconciled.

27 Work It

The manager's role on the team

It's one thing for managers to tell staff how to do the right things. It's quite another to show them. The role of your managers and assistant managers on both the front-of-the-house and kitchen teams is to model effective team behavior.

Want your team members to communicate well, treat each other with respect and help each other out whenever possible? That's what your managers will have to do for them in exchange.

Managers who stand back critiquing employees' performance when members of the team are in need of help hamper your team-building efforts. It sends a message that they're somehow superior to the rest of the team. You don't need generals. You need all the front-line troopers you can get to help meet your operation's goals.

Managers should be visible to employees. Leave paperwork in the office until a time when the pace slows down enough for employees to handle their responsibilities.

They should model the way. On the floor, that means meeting the needs of every guest in every section when they see opportunities to help out. It means busing tables, running food orders out, picking up trash on the floor – everything employees are expected to do for one another.

In the kitchen, their role is back-up for any team member who needs it. That means rolling up their sleeves and mopping up messes, if that's the task at hand.

But that's not to say employees are off the hook. Managers should hold employees accountable for their individual tasks. A manager who is pre-busing tables and running food orders out for a server who's out having a quick smoke break is not helping the team.

To do all this, your managers and assistant managers must be properly trained in every task of your restaurant. Require that every manager participate in monthly and pre-shift meetings for their respective teams – not as team leaders, but as team members. Just because they have the rank doesn't mean they're the best choice to lead the team. But you will want them to be on the same page with their teammates.

TIP

Power to the People

Managers shouldn't take over on the floor. If a guest has a problem with his or her meal or service, encourage servers to solve it themselves rather than running for you or another manager. First, train them with the proper techniques for handling customer complaints. And let them know that you will back up any action they take to please the guest. Allow them to take matters into their own hands within the guidelines you set – whether it means comping menu items, making substitutions or making other amends to satisfy the customer. Empowering your employees to solve problems not only encourages them to take more responsibility for their guests' dining experiences, it also sends a powerful message to your guests – it says you have full faith in the people who will be providing their service.

28 Give It Up

Delegating management tasks to employee teams

From marketing and promotions to purchasing and cost control, your employees have abilities well beyond their job descriptions. Why not ease your management load by delegating management tasks to employee teams?

When managers delegate, their employees get better training and more responsibility, while getting involved in the decision making for the whole operation. They have greater enthusiasm about working for you and take more initiative in other areas. Efficiency and productivity increase and, by making better use of your resources, you spend more time on other management tasks.

Form "special teams" to solve your biggest problems. For example, compile a safety committee to review accidents that have occurred in the past and find ways to prevent similar incidents. Have team members do their homework to become safety experts and give safety talks at staff training meetings. Encourage them to come up with lively, entertaining presentations and conceive creative incentives to help the staff "think safety."

Have a quality-control team explore ways to ensure guests always receive the best you have to offer. Encourage members to challenge your traditional systems to come up with new and better ways of doing things. Once the team creates a new system, put the members in charge of implementing it and training the appropriate staff.

Give up management tasks that will help an existing team with their regular tasks. For example, perhaps you could have prep cooks take over purchasing and receiving tasks. It's already part of their job to know about recipe ingredients and food shelf lives. You'll just be giving their jobs a little more dimension, keeping them from becoming mundane. You'll need to train them carefully for this important duty, but the extra training time will pay off in the long run.

Allow your employees to get involved in the day-to-day operation of your restaurant by assigning them tasks that apply to their chosen careers. Most restaurants employ more than a few college students. Put together, for example, a marketing team. Have a marketing major help plan your next promotion. Solicit the help of an aspiring graphic artist to design flyers and advertising for the event. Have a public relations student work on getting media coverage. Have a music major audition and hire bands for live performances.

A Delegator's Checklist

Many managers resist delegating because they lack confidence in their employees' abilities, or they feel that it would be quicker to just do it themselves. But giving employees added responsibilities is important for both their individual growth and development of the team. Some tips:

- **Decide what to delegate to which groups. Consider skill, motivation and workload. Match skills and interests with tasks.**
- **Don't watch over their shoulders. Agree beforehand how and when you'll be checking progress.**
- **Discuss clear goals and performance standards – and possible pitfalls.**
- **Develop a good attitude. Trust employees to get the job done, even if experience is lacking.**
- **Compare results with goals. Discuss and give feedback.**

29 The Idea Mill

Generating business solutions with team suggestions

> **"'I must do something' will solve more problems than 'something must be done.'"**
> — *Roxanne K. Pishnick, T.G.I. Friday's*

The best way to get employees past a problem is to get them involved in the solution. Build a better working environment by involving all of your staff in the decision-making for your operation. You'll ease your management team's workload and show employees that their ideas are not only encouraged, but valued.

If you have a problem with poor service, soaring costs or low sales, present the challenges to your employees at an all-staff meeting. Break them into teams and ask *smart* questions like, "What can we change to improve our service, lower our costs and increase our sales?" or "What are some of the reasons we're experiencing these problems now?" People don't argue with their own data.

Encourage them to brainstorm as many solutions as possible in 15 minutes. Award the team generating the most ideas with individual one-dollar lotto quick-picks for their "million-dollar" contributions.

The tried-and-true suggestion box could be put to work for generating great ideas. But many managers have given them up because they find nothing more than gum wrappers dropped through the slot. That's often because those employees who've made suggestions in the past have never heard them acknowledged. To put a suggestion box to use most effectively, consider an incentive to employees who feed the box the greatest quantity of useful ideas. Come up with a new theme every week.

For added motivation, award additional prizes for implementation. Once you've approved the idea, encourage the employee to assemble a team to help him or her implement the idea. Recognize any contribution this team makes. Whether their ideas solve your biggest problems or not, your employees are taking the initiative to work in a team. That means you've achieved success in building a positive team environment.

Great Idea, But ...

Sometimes you have to disapprove of a team's ideas and decisions. How do you say no without turning players off of the entire team concept? Give them a detailed explanation. Not everyone will be happy with your decision, but at least they'll understand your rationale. Raise issues about the idea that concern you, and let them address those, too. When people talk things through, they usually begin to see the light. And if they don't, *you* may be wrong. Before you veto a team's ideas or decisions, be sure your reasons are valid. The worst thing a manager can do is turn down a suggestion with no discussion, because then your people will never share their ideas again.

> "In baseball, as in business, a game won today will count as much as a game won at the end of the season."
> — *Johnny Bench*

CHAPTER THREE:
Practice Makes Perfect

The success of a team can be measured by the success of a team's practices. Natural talent may take you far, but ultimate success is achieved by those who train every day. Your restaurant teams will perform best if they can take a few tips from the professional sports world: Practice makes perfect.

Sure, training will cost you a little more time, money and effort in the short run. But the more you expect from your employees, the more you have to train them.

On the pages that follow, we'll explore the importance of teamwork training – how to become better communicators, problem solvers and mentors. And we'll discuss some more advanced team-building concepts like evaluating team effectiveness, overcoming obstacles and managing conflicts.

30 No Train? No Gain!

The importance of training

> "The more you expect from a person, the more you have to train them."
> — *Geoff Bailey, Colorado Restaurateur*

"If only we could act more like a team." It's a common mantra of restaurant operators. But saying it and making it happen are on opposite banks of the river. And if your staff still isn't working together effectively, you have a bit of paddling to do. Teamwork doesn't happen overnight. It takes time, planning and a dedication to ongoing staff training.

At great restaurants, training is a philosophy, not a department. Your employees are your most important resource. Recognize them by training and re-training them monthly, daily – even hourly, customizing your approach to suit every greeter, server, bartender, buser, cook and dishwasher.

A well-trained staff not only helps your employees improve hard skills, like operating kitchen equipment, busing tables and mixing drinks, it helps you improve soft skills, like communication, leadership and trust. Which, by the way, are the essential elements of teamwork.

Effective training begins with preparation. Decide what your sales, service and productivity goals are, then use your training sessions to communicate those goals to everyone on your staff. Base your training on the behavior you expect and not just attitude. Your staff can have the best attitude in the world, but if their behavior doesn't match your objectives, there's no improvement.

They say it takes 21 days of different behavior to change a habit. That's why training *daily* is critical. Use monthly staff meetings for broader topics and implement daily pre-shift team meetings by department for quick refreshers and mini-training sessions.

Make sure everyone gets involved. Either through participating in training exercises, keeping up a lively dialogue or leading a training session, everyone on the staff should speak once during every session.

And stop ranting about "acting more like a team." Until you show your staff *how*, you won't get the results you're after.

TIP

How Much Is a Guest Worth?

"But training time is money," say most operators who complain that they have no time for regular staff training. Consider the costs of subjecting your guests to an untrained staff. What if bad service drives a customer away? The dollar cost of losing just one guest may not seem like much, but imagine the alternative: What if your well-trained, team-oriented staff provides such *good* service, that same guest comes in once a week instead of once a month, bringing his friends and family along? What if your well-trained server convinces him to always order a premium liquor in his cocktails and order an appetizer? Effective staff training will make you or break you.

Meeting Needs

Effective training meetings

Training meetings are often like a dentist chair for teams – a painful place team members would like to avoid. They'll hurt a lot less if you use basic rules of meeting discipline:

- Make the most of your training time by creating a meeting environment that encourages everyone to participate.

- Keep distractions to a minimum. Don't hold meetings in high-traffic areas in your restaurant. And don't hold them facing windows.

- Don't use what little training time you have to drone on about dress codes, policies and procedures. That's why most managers and staffers hate training and why most sessions fail to communicate any valuable skills employees can use on the floor. Nothing lasts as long as a box of cereal you don't like and a training session you can't stand.

- Keep them short – no more than 90 minutes, once a month. Any longer is a waste of time – and employees will come to resent them.

- Have an agenda with three or four items to be covered.

- Create dialogue, not monologue. Use this opportunity to exchange ideas, test skills and solicit feedback.

> **"The greatest enemy of training in the classroom is preoccupation or distraction. The greatest enemy of training outside the classroom is habit."**
> — *Bob Pike*

- Be sure all training is performance-based: The focus should always be on what the employee will be able to do as a result of the training.

- Remember that meetings provide time for team members to report on their progress and problems. Give them time to celebrate successes and hash out solutions when necessary.

Lighten Up

Make your training fun, lively and relevant. Appeal to all the senses by using fun visual aids like flip charts and colorful markers, props, videos and work-books, flash cards and little tokens, like lotto tickets or dollar bills, to reward participation. Use role-play sessions to help test the newly learned skills and follow up on the floor, providing constant feedback as employees develop their skills.

32 Open Communication

Training staff to become better communicators

If your employees can't talk to each other effectively, how can you expect them to work together effectively? Communication breakdown is the number-one hindrance to teambuilding. And the two factors that separate effective teams from the ineffective ones are the abilities of team members to actively listen to one another and respond in a positive manner. Unfortunately, these two areas often get more lip service than action.

Teach your staff that their most important listening skill is the ability to sit back, be attentive and take in what is said without passing judgment. People can absorb and process words spoken by other people much faster than they can verbalize the information. This leaves a lot of time to analyze, evaluate and even anticipate the speaker's thoughts. People tend to concentrate less on what's being said and too often discount comments even before they are completed.

Teach your staff how to be active listeners. Stress the importance of body language: Active listeners nod, maintain eye contact and lean forward. They also add short verbal acknowledgments such as "I see" and "Uh huh."

Active listening is all the more powerful because it so rarely happens. When someone really listens, the speaker is doubly impressed – with him- or herself and with the other person. The person is saying "I'm interested in what you have to say."

Active listeners also show the speaker they're interested and attentive by paraphrasing expressed facts and feelings. Sometimes called reflecting, the classic response begins, "What I hear you saying is ..." Or "You seem upset about ..." The active listener's goal is to make sure he or she is clear about what is intended and to let the speaker know you care about what's being communicated.

Powerful Positive Speaking

Ever wondered how some people always achieve their goals? The secret to their success may lie within their manner of speaking – it's positive. Teach your staff to wipe out the negativity in their daily speech by using these alternatives. They can help improve communication on every level:

Instead of:	Say this:
I'll have to ...	I'll be glad to ...
I can't ...	I haven't yet ...
I should have ...	Starting now, I will ...
What's wrong with...	How can we improve ...
I disagree ...	I understand how you feel ...

33 When Worlds Collide

Crossing cultural road blocks with diversity training

When corporate America talks of "going global," it's usually a sign of success. The restaurant industry has been "global" for some time, with the never-ending draw for employees attracting people from all walks of life, all corners of the world. But the language and cultural barriers that come with the diversified workforce have resulted in a great deal of tension for operators. The tension is especially apparent when it comes to improving teamwork. How do you build staff unity and mutual respect when often they can't even communicate with each other?

The first step is changing mindsets. When it comes to team-building, it's the diversity of ideas that's important, not the diversity of employees. It's not just about language. It's about respecting everyone on the staff. When you can switch the focus from gender, race, sexual preference and religion to concentrate instead on creating a culture that enables *all* employees to reach their full potential, you create a team that works together for the company's success.

Invest in diversity training materials for all your employees. Outline what you deem acceptable behavior. Not only will diversity training help them respect each other, it may help you avoid a discrimination suit.

Teach them about each other's native countries. It's not a language barrier, it's a cultural barrier. And culture clashes often manifest into needling little problems that could easily be avoided with an understanding of the way things are done "back where I'm from."

Help foreign-language-speaking employees communicate by teaching them a little English. Or meet their individual needs by helping those employees schedule work hours around English classes.

Better yet, hold basic foreign-language classes for all your English-speaking employees, focusing on the words and phrases they'll need to use every shift. It's a sign of respect to learn someone's native tongue – and foreign staffers will reciprocate by practicing more English. Pretty soon they'll all be learning from each other.

What do you stand to lose? When you ignore the needs of people of different cultures, religions and lifestyles, they feel misunderstood, unappreciated and, worse, isolated – and that's a tough atmosphere for growing feelings of teamwork and loyalty.

Achieving Diversity

A few other things you can do to help your diverse staff work together:

- **For hiring, learn to effectively interview people from cultures other than your own.**
- **Watch the social interaction between your staff members to see if some employees are being excluded or offended.**
- **If it appears some are, ask them, "How do you feel you're treated here?" and "What can I do to help?"**
- **For contests and incentives, group employees into teams made up of people with race, gender or other differences – and coach them on working together effectively.**
- **Involve *all* employees in decisions that until now have been made only by management.**

34 Trust Me

Creating trust

"Everyone on my staff is so polite to one another," say managers. "But still, nobody's helping one another, and tasks fall through the cracks while customers are left unserved."

No matter how "polite" they are, too often there are conflicts that exist. Many employees are thinking, "Why should I help my co-workers when they never help me?" Teamwork requires knowing – without a doubt – that someone will always be there to back you up.

Trust in a relationship is a fragile thing. It doesn't come quickly – we tend to withhold trust until others prove themselves worthy of it – and yet it can be destroyed by one simple violation. There are three levels of trust: 1. *High trust.* When this exists, people show little concern about getting their share because they know that the other parties will not take advantage of them. 2. *Low trust.* People in these relationships are preoccupied with seeing that they get their fair share and that the other parties get no more. 3. *No trust.* People who have lost all trust live by the motto, "I'm going to get them before they get me."

Here are some tips to help your teams reach level one:

Spend time together: Trust develops when people get to know one another. Host regular staff or team get-togethers where employees can socialize.

Create opportunities for people to work together: Strive to design work so that people have to collaborate. For example, make cleaning larger appliances a two-person job.

Improve communication. Members of the team must have confidence that they can reveal aspects of themselves and their work without fear of reprisals or embarrassment.

Encourage discussion of problems and key issues: It must be seen as OK to ask for help or to seek the advice of other team members.

Be personal: Encourage staffers to use first-person language in describing their work. "I am ... " "I feel ..." "I think ..." And encourage them to ask each other "emotive" questions like, "How do you feel about ...?" "What is your opinion of ...?"

Give it time: When a new team forms, typically the level of trust is low. While polite, employees are still testing each other. But as the team matures, trust will often automatically increase. They need to regularly witness team member helping team member before they can make that leap of trust.

Use positive reinforcement: When the team first forms, reward contributions by team members: Those who pitch in for others, are dependable, share views, etc. Provide ongoing feedback to each member individually.

Trust Busters

Share the following list of trust-breaking behaviors with your staff:

- **Ignoring people**
- **Embarrassing someone in front of the group**
- **Failing to keep a confidence**
- **Avoiding eye contact**
- **Withholding credit when it's due**
- **Interrupting when others are talking**
- **Withholding help when you're clearly not busy**
- **Taking over someone else's tasks when that person can handle them**
- **Breaking a promise.**

35 By All Accounts

Establishing individual accountability

"Nobody cares what I do until I don't do it," complain many of your employees. When it comes to building teams, however, everyone should care about what everyone does.

Every member of the team has his or her own responsibilities, and the success of the team hinges on their completion. When one member of the team fails to carry the load, the entire team suffers.

By definition, effective teams hold themselves mutually accountable for achieving the team's goals. Members must also hold themselves individually accountable. Otherwise, your team members' trust in one another is compromised.

How do you teach employees to hold themselves accountable for their own actions? How do you encourage employees to set high performance standards for themselves?

Start by disciplining employees for low performance. If you're going to reward good team behavior, you must also set conditions for poor behavior. This means making clear and consistent demands that reflect the needs of customers and other team members. Be sure every employee is fully aware of all the essential functions of his or her job – and is trained properly to handle the job.

Pinpointing performance problems requires identifying what people do, not what they don't do. Managers often say, "Don't make errors," "Don't have accidents," "Don't be late." Keep in mind that people are hired to *do* things. Active behavior gets things done. If someone is making mistakes, telling the person to stop making errors will not solve the problem because one way of not making errors is to do nothing. If you tell kitchen employees to stop wasting food with misprepared orders, they will inevitably begin burying their mistakes in the nearest waste basket. But give that kitchen staffer the opportunity to tell you why he thinks he made the mistake, and you can work with the employee to find the source of the problem – and look for solutions.

Making Mistakes

Accidents will happen. Mistakes will be made. Nobody's perfect. Learning from mishaps, though, can be the difference between a high-performance team and just a group of people working together. People can't just hold themselves accountable to positive behaviors. They must be made to feel comfortable in openly confessing mistakes. It builds trust within the team, and the team can't succeed without that. Going overboard with demands for perfection encourages employees to hide the problems, sweep mistakes under the rug and blame others. Conversely, creating a culture where people feel comfortable 'fessing up to their goofs makes everyone feel a common bond. And identifying problems is the only way the team can get to the bottom of them.

36 Great Beginnings

Team-building begins at orientation

> **"An employee is never more focused, malleable and teachable than the first day on the job."**
> — *Horst Schulze, CEO, Ritz-Carlton Hotels*

Communicate your team philosophy to new hires from their first day on the job. After all, this initial period is when they're forming the behaviors and attitudes they'll carry through their entire employment at your restaurant.

Begin training them to be a part of the team the minute they walk in the door and be sure the training is effective – you'll never have a better chance to teach them right. And if they go out on their first shift without the knowledge to do the job, their team members may develop a resentment that will be hard to break later on.

New employees will be a bit nervous on their first day, so you and your trainers should make every effort to put them at ease. Walk them around the restaurant, introducing them to every team player you see.

If you've hired several people for new positions, have them go through at least part of their orientation together – even if they're training for different positions. There's strength in numbers! They'll develop camaraderie with their new teammates and gain a clearer understanding of their role as they learn about other positions.

As soon as possible, explain to new hires the importance of their individual positions and how they fit into the big picture. Your enthusiasm at this point will raise interest in their new jobs and roles on the team.

Set high standards when training. You can't expect new employees to do a first-class job after seeing a second-class demonstration. As you train, make the new employee feel free to ask questions. If they're not asking questions, they may not be understanding what you're teaching them.

Give reasons for methods and procedures in layman's terms – this applies to both the "telling" and the "showing" part of training. Your new employees will learn more easily and remember longer if they can attach meaning to the tasks. Teach skills that can be performed immediately so your hires can feel productive on their first day.

Avoid criticism. Instead, show new employees a better way to do their tasks. Your praise and encouragement will help build their self-confidence. And be sure to follow up, checking each trainee's performance as often as possible.

The Welcome Wagon

Take the team approach to orientation by involving everyone on staff in the new employee's training. Have department leaders conduct brief training sessions for new hires. These sessions should be upbeat and positive while detailing how the employee's job responsibilities will coincide with the other department's. For instance, new servers should each spend some time behind the bar learning the ins and outs of the bartender's world. Other stops might include the host stand, cashier area, kitchen, etc. The broader the understanding, the more effective the employee will be later on.

37 One on One

Mentors help integrate new hires into the team

> **"Train today for tomorrow. It wasn't raining when Noah built the ark."**
> — *Howard Ruff*

It's the lowest-common-denominator theory at work: Your low-performing team players bring the performance of the entire team down to their level. Other employees on the team will resent being asked to help out their teammates if they feel they're having to work harder to compensate for a low-performing employee's poor work habits.

And much of the problem could be traced back to the training room. When an employee is poorly trained at orientation, his or her sub-par work habits hinder the team's progress toward its goals.

To maintain high-performance standards throughout the team, assign an experienced team player to serve as the new employee's mentor during the first few weeks on the job. This provides the new hire with a role model not only in terms of the work, but also in terms of his or her development as a team player.

Plus, it helps the new hire feel like a part of the team from the very beginning.

Mentors should condition new team members to believe that they're joining an elite group – that the team is made up of winners, and they wouldn't be there if they weren't winners, too.

And for the mentor, the experience provides the best chance of ensuring the job gets done right – during training and later on the shift. It's up to the mentor to be sure the new hire's job skills will be in line with what the rest of the group needs. When we teach, we learn twice.

Assign a Shepherd

Offer mentors a bonus after 30 or 60 days if the new employee stays with the restaurant at least a month and has above-average performance over that time period. Why? The bonus helps the trainer "shepherd" the trainee into better skills over the first month of employment and is an effective reward that encourages improvement in teaching skills. Have the shepherd review new hires' progress with them weekly to ensure their skills are improving. When you get employees involved in the teaching, you also get them involved in the learning.

(38) Across the Board

Cross-training

> "Never learn to do anything. If you don't learn, you'll always find someone else to do it."
> — *Mark Twain*

Nothing brings things into perspective like a walk in someone else's shoes. Cross-training employees will become one of your strongest team-building techniques because it helps employees see the challenges faced by their peers.

If you were a dishwasher and then became a buser, no one would have to tell you that it helps to throw out leftovers, separate glasses and put knives on top. You'd already know how much it helped – and you'd do it, *without* being asked.

By cross-training members of your kitchen crew, they'll learn new skills that will keep their jobs from becoming mundane. And, should your line cook call in sick, you won't be wiped out for the shift since you'll be able to rotate your prep cook in to cover the orders.

A buser who's been cross-trained in the server's responsibilities can help run orders out to guests and answer questions about the menu. Put them through sales training, as well, so they'll be able to upsell guests who ask for menu suggestions.

Cross-training offers you scheduling flexibility, too. Say you've already scheduled all your dishwashers for 40 hours and you still need someone for Saturday night. Instead of paying overtime, maybe there's a buser who's looking for some extra hours. By placing employees in different positions, you'll be able to show them their place in the big picture.

Combine a cross-training program with incentives. Begin employees at a training wage and award raises for learning a new function. Start servers as busers and after weeks of working in all positions, including the kitchen, finally promote them to waiting on tables.

Is it worth the extra training time? No doubt about it. Cross-training ultimately results in a loyal staff because they understand the restaurant's system and are aware of what is happening in each facet of the operation.

TIP Moving On Up

Cross-training can also be an important job perk. Your employees will appreciate your efforts to help them increase their job skills – and the opportunity for a promotion. So when hiring, be on the lookout for candidates who have the potential to be cross-trained. It takes a special kind of person to take the initiative to learn a new job. You need to choose carefully because you're investing time and training in these special people. During the interview, ask employees how they feel about accepting new responsibilities. And push them to elaborate. "Which types of responsibilities would you want to take on?" "What other positions would you be interested in preparing for?" Begin cross-training immediately so when a position opens, the employee will be ready to start. You cut down on the hiring and orientation costs of hiring someone from the outside.

39 Show Me the Way

The art of effective role-playing

As the old Chinese proverb goes: "I hear and I forget, I see and I remember, I do and I understand." One of the best ways to get your employees to work together effectively is to have them practice together effectively. To make the most of your training time, put your team members "in the driver's seat" where they can try out their new skills.

Add role-playing sessions to every pre-shift, monthly or quarterly meeting. This effective technique will help teams reinforce training on every front-line employee's customer service-related tasks – from suggestive selling and learning guest names to product knowledge and providing smiling, friendly service.

More important, by letting them role-play their new skills on their teammates, everyone on the team can evaluate the employees' mastery of those skills *before* they head out to the floor.

Training Principles 101 taught us that people learn best by doing. Still, many managers and team leaders believe all they need to do at training sessions is be a good speaker and scribble on a flip chart. Sure, that's all part of it. But think back to how you learned to drive and you'll see why role-playing is so important. Did you have someone explain it on a flip chart then jump into a $50,000 hot rod? Probably not.

Most of us had someone *show* us the proper techniques. Then we practiced over and over – on wet roads, on dry roads, in traffic, on open highways – until we felt confident enough with our skills to drive the DMV heavy around the block a few times. It wasn't until after *he* gave us the green light that someone handed us the keys to the hot rod.

Effective role-playing in five easy steps

TIP

1. Write scenarios on note cards in advance and write out customer dialogue on "cheat sheets."

2. On a flip chart, write three specific behaviors, like upselling, learning guests names and offering a choice.

3. Call up role-players one scenario at a time. Don't just pick good servers or bad servers. Give everyone on the team a chance.

4. Afterward, critique by asking the team: "What, if anything, could she have done better?" Detail any missed opportunities.

5. Review the main points and ask the team "What are you going to do differently as a result of today's training?"

40 Quality Time

Effective management teams

> "If we're all thinking alike, somebody isn't thinking."
> — *General George Patton*

When it comes to management teams, few GM's will admit that what they really want is a group of "yes men" who think and feel exactly the way they do. It's human nature to seek out similar personalities – people whose philosophies and work ethics complement your own.

But be careful. By ignoring other points of view, you reduce the chance to find creative solutions to your biggest problems and new ideas for the future. No business can function if everyone thinks exactly alike. Creative solutions require thinking outside the box.

Treat your managers as valuable members of your operations team. Doing so will set the tone for how they treat the rest of the staff. So if you truly want their help in building a team culture, you'll need to give up some control.

Encourage those managers who think differently from yourself to speak up, even openly disagreeing with your orders. Eliminate any job security fears they may have in doing so. By prizing diverse ideas, you'll add to your own and strengthen the overall operation.

At the end of each of your management meetings, set aside a few minutes for a group discussion on the quality of the meeting's interactions. Was the group able to work together to find solutions to problems? Focus the discussion on what went well and what needs improving. Who dominated? Who said nothing? Who helped the discussion? Did anyone hinder the discussion? What can be done the next time to make the meeting better? Honesty is the key – don't get taken in by yes-people. Conversely, if you sense that *you* are a part of the problem, ask your other managers for ways you can become a part of the solution. It often helps if someone else chairs the meeting. Better yet, consider rotating the chair among other managers on your team.

TIP

Yes, Sir

How do you know when your managers have gotten over the hump, making valuable contributions rather than "yessing" everything you say or do? They...

- **address you no more formally than they do others in the group.**
- **don't look to you to start the meeting (or end it).**
- **speak up spontaneously without asking your permission.**
- **start to disagree with you or question your opinions.**
- **arrive at decisions without checking with you as the final judge.**
- **utilize the experience of others rather than depend on yours alone.**
- **play an active role in making contributions that improve function.**
- **confront other members who are disrupting the group or hindering progress rather than look to you to confront them.**

Brain Waves

Brainstorming techniques

When you solicit the help of employee or management teams to solve your operation's toughest problems, you'll want the most innovative solutions they can come up with. Follow these tips to help generate the best ideas.

- State the target clearly. For example, ask, "How can we increase customer traffic?" or "How can we motivate employees to keep the place clean?"

- Few issues have just one right answer. The solution is usually found in a range of possibilities. The challenge for your group is to find the one that best fits the environment in which it will have to survive. Policies, funding, timing and staffing are some examples of these environmental conditions.

- Quantity counts. Ask members to come up with as many ideas as they can, as quickly as they can.

- No criticism is allowed. Tell the group that there are no impossible ideas at this stage and the crazier the better.

- Involve everyone. Let each member participate in their own way and in a manner that makes them feel comfortable.

> **"A moment's insight is sometimes worth a life's experience."**
> — *Oliver Wendell Holmes*

- Assign two people with the task of "recorder," but remind them not to interfere when the ideas start flying. This will ensure that everything is captured in the group memory. Halfway through, switch recorders to alter the makeup of the group.

- Stay out of the way when a group takes off and "free-thinks" in all directions – no matter how wacky the session becomes.

- If the group bogs down, have the recorders review the list of ideas to help the group think of variations. Build on the ideas of others. Ask them to flip ideas over, propose the opposite, add to them and piggy-back on others' ideas.

- Constantly encourage and reward the group.

Outside the Box

Often groups have difficulty thinking beyond what they know to be true today. When the group gets stuck, it needs your guidance to expand its horizons and think creatively. Generating ideas is a lot like childhood imagination games. And most of us are too far away from childhood to remember what that feels like. Encourage participants to close their eyes and think back to those rainy, nothing-to-do days when they let their imaginations take over. How did it feel? Can you achieve that feeling again? Some will resist, since playing has become synonymous with not working. Having fun is essential now – and it is legitimate work!

42 What's the Problem?

Problem solving to improve team effectiveness

Few teams develop in a straightforward fashion. When teams encounter stress – say, when they lose or add new members, lose trust or lose sight of their goals – they must go through a problem-solving stage to get back on track.

Problems a team encounters generally fall into one of three categories: technical problems, systems problems or people-related problems.

Most team problems are either technical or systemic, but teams tend to misidentify most of them as people-related.

To solve problems effectively, teams need a structured process to identify root causes, then generate and implement the best possible solutions. Teams also need a variety of problem-solving tools to deal with specific problems.

Encourage your teams to go through this five-step process when a problem arises:

1. Discuss and define the problem. Say, for example, two members of the team are bickering over whose responsibility it is to perform a certain task.

2. Determine the problem's root cause. In this case, it's probably caused by an unclear definition of work roles and task assignments.

3. Generate possible solutions. Assign the task to one team member's job description, and let others know they may be expected to complete the task if their time allows.

4. Recommend, approve and implement a solution. Team members should put the new task assignments to work on the next shift.

5. Measure and evaluate the results of the solution – and give team members time to adjust. After a few weeks, bring up the topic at a training meeting. Is the task being completed – without grumbling – by the employee? Are other employees helping out when they can?

TIP Red Alert

Here are some signs that a team is struggling:

- **Members cannot easily describe the team's mission.**

- **Relations are formal, stuffy or tense.**

- **There is talk but not much communication.**

- **Disagreements are aired in private conversations instead of in the open.**

- **There is confusion or disagreement about roles or task assignments.**

- **Decisions tend to be made by the formal leader with little meaningful involvement from other team members.**

- **Members are not open with each other because trust is low.**

42 I Did It My Way

Recognizing different work styles

Slow and steady may win some races, but it loses others. People have different work styles, and when you put them in teams, members with different styles must learn to work side-by-side.

Work styles have to do with pace, detail orientation, job skills and flexibility. How people work reflects both their personality and the way they were trained. Were you taught to maintain a fast pace, dealing with errors later on? Or were you rewarded for getting it right the first time, even when it meant going slower and working more carefully? Did you work in an operation in which safety and quality were top priorities, or were speed and volume emphasized?

For instance, all servers will complete their sidework at different paces. If you require the quick ones to help out the slow ones after finishing their own duties, you'll create resentment.

Or if one buser is a perfectionist on setting up tables and another's a speed demon who's a little sloppy, you'll have trouble holding them accountable to the same quality control standards. They both have their value in different situations, but they can't be compared.

Conflicts about work styles surface more quickly in teams than among individuals working independently. When output depends upon each team member taking responsibility for a share of the work, work styles affect productivity –

which can influence whether the team reaches its goals.

While there is room for different work styles in most of your teams, minimum requirements must be set to avoid conflict. Pace and work quality are standards that must be maintained equally by all team members, while preferences for different kinds of work can often be met by rotating jobs. Sometimes the range of jobs allows for different work styles, but shuffling off the less-demanding jobs on the slower or less-skilled workers can create resentment.

One For All ...

Here's how to be sure different work styles don't destroy the team effort:

- **Maintain standards. There is really only one solution to the issue of different work styles: Have the same performance standards for everyone. Equal performance fosters mutual respect in teams.**

- **Balance the demands of different jobs. If team members rotate through several jobs, don't make some so hard or others so easy and desirable that they become, respectively, punishment or light duty.**

- **Encourage respect for different styles through training. Make sure people understand that it's OK to do things differently, provided everyone maintains consistently high work standards.**

43 Conflicting Emotions

Managing conflicts between teams

Why can't we all just get along? Because we're all different people and when things get hectic, we all react differently. Conflicts most commonly occur between departments – kitchen employees vs. servers, dishwashers vs. busers, servers vs. bartenders, etc. The first step for you is to understand that these conflicts will occur – no matter what.

For example, front-of-the-house and "heart"-of-the-house employees will always be at odds because they work in two completely different worlds. Understand the kitchen staffers' perspective – from their sweaty perches in the back so far removed from the guests, they forget that servers get in the weeds just like they do. They rarely see a guest yelling at a server. All they see are servers in the back socializing with one another while they wait for orders. And servers have a nasty habit of wiping their "serving smiles" off their faces as soon as they barrel through the kitchen door, snarling at the head cook about a remake on an order.

A simple "please" and "thank you" could help, but these wounds run much deeper. What most really want is courtesy and understanding from the other teams. But what they often get are sneers.

The problems arise when the conflicts aren't resolved satisfactorily. Long-term grievances set in and communication breakdowns get even worse. Here's how to help staff resolve their differences:

The first hurdle in conflict resolution is the toughest for most managers: Encourage disagreements. They are the natural consequences of a dynamic, active organization. Without them, you can be assured that people aren't saying what's really on their minds. Conflicts can be destructive or constructive. Don't sweep them under the rug. Acknowledging disagreements is the first step toward solving them.

Make sure everyone has good basic team skills: The ability to ask and answer questions, practice active listening, convey information, provide feedback and get along with others. Go back to the training room if they don't.

Ask: "How are we doing?" Encourage the team to use a climate survey periodically to measure its own morale and, yes, "team spirit."

Create a norm for politeness and respect by discussing good behavior and seeking and rewarding examples of it.

Seek peer feedback during performance reviews. This can be a real eye-opener both within and between teams. Get individuals to rate the people they work with in such categories as output, quality, cooperation and knowledge.

Face Off

Encourage inter-team relations by having members "face off" to solve problems. For example, gather your front-of-the-house team together and explain the kitchen perspective on their world. Do the same with the kitchen team. Then call them all together. Have them face off in chairs across from each other. Going down the line, have members of each group voice grievances about the other. Then go back down the line and have each member suggest a solution to any problem that was brought up. Encourage them to focus on changes to the work system, not just suggest changes in attitude. Use the list of solutions as the starting block for a group discussion. Don't look just to compromise. If the teams aren't happy with the outcome, keep plugging through the issues until they are.

44 Quitting Time

Dealing with turnover

Sometimes it may seem like the labor pool is shrinking, since it's so hard to find good employees who'll stick around. At the same time, new restaurants are opening at a rabbit's pace. If you think you're having staffing trouble now, where will you be in three years?

Turnover is an ongoing restaurant reality. And, yes, it will have a negative effect on the team. When a member leaves, it messes up your team's basic dynamic. A new employee must be oriented to the group, which takes time.

And at its most basic level, turnover forces team members to lose trust: "I trusted that she would always be there to back me up. Now she's gone ..."

When a good employee leaves, managers and leaders will probably have to do some damage control. First, put a positive spin on the employee's departure. If the employee is leaving on good terms for a better opportunity, have him or her explain that to the team. Team members should be encouraged not to take offense. They should wish departing employees well, treating them like ambassadors rather than rebels.

If the employee is leaving on bad terms, explain what those terms are to staff. Watching someone they're close to get fired or quit angrily is very unsettling to teammates. They'll wonder if their individual behavior is leading them down the same path.

Be honest about the reasons for the team member's departure. It will stop employee gossip before it starts.

Remind team members that the departure does not necessarily reflect badly on the team. Encourage them to accept the dynamic nature of a restaurant workplace. Help team members view the turnover as a positive. Here's a chance to do some refocusing. Steer teams back through the stages of development outlined earlier. And perhaps the replacement team member will be an even more effective performer.

Learning from Mistakes

Face it: You can't keep good people forever in the restaurant business. Many people simply pass through on their way to other careers. Learn from the experience by holding exit interviews with all departing employees. It's a great way to find out what they really think of your operation, team structure and management style. Ask things like, "What did you like about working here?" "What didn't you like?" and "Based on your experience here, what qualities do you think your replacement should have?" Her answers will tell you what you're doing right – things you'll want to continue doing to incorporate other good employees into the team.

45 Forward March

Challenging teams to improve

> **"Go as far as you can see and when you get there you will see farther."**
> — *Early American Proverb*

Because many people achieve goals to avoid punishment, they often do no more than they're asked to. If you positively reinforce their success, however, they'll do their best to keep on getting that positive reinforcement.

Challenge teams to improve their performance by setting their first goal slightly ahead of their level, and measure success daily or weekly. It won't take long for reinforced people to reach the ultimate goal.

Set low goals and raise them gradually. Low goals increase the odds of success. When management celebrates each time a goal is reached, people are reinforced to exceed that goal the next time.

Goals set the stage for positive reinforcement, so the more goals you have, the more opportunities you'll have for positive reinforcement. A few lofty goals that are hard to reach can be counterproductive. They'll decrease opportunities for positive reinforcement, rewards and celebrations.

Managers who make positive reinforcement a way of life inject six basic values into the workplace.

1. Honesty. Keep your motives pure. Make sure people understand why you're asking for a certain behavior. In your case, you want to increase profits.

2. Integrity. This is the basis for trust. Make sure that what you say will happen after a certain behavior or perfor-

mance actually does happen. People must believe that you say what you mean and mean what you say.

3. Justice. Ensure that people will get what they deserve. Those who perform well should get more than those who perform poorly.

4. Self-esteem and personal growth. Provide reinforcement and rewards that give performers tangible proof that they add value to your operation. The experience will enhance their initiative and encourage them to try new ideas.

5. Personal security. Make sure people know exactly which behaviors you want and what the consequences of those behaviors will be.-This is a major step toward alleviating mental confusion and stress.

6. When positive reinforcement becomes a way of life in an organization, adversarial relationships begin to disappear. People start to treat each other as they would like to be treated. In such an atmosphere, employees learn that they can earn bigger rewards by working together than they could by resisting each other. Work becomes a pleasant win/win experience and a cause for celebration.

Keeping Score

One critical difference between a group and a team is that a team knows what constitutes a win. But you have to let members know how close they are to a win and what they need to do to make that win happen. Put up scoreboards where everyone on staff can see them. Examples may include "102 days since our last accident," "3,240 happy customers," "524 appetizers sold," or "257 orders filled without a mistake." Your team needs to have something that represents a winning score. Otherwise, employees may work for weeks and months and never know if they've won or lost. Update your scoreboards constantly. They will also serve as trophies to show off successes to your other staff teams.

IV

"My idea of discipline is not makin' guys do something. It's gettin' 'em to do it. There's a difference in bitchin' and coachin'."
— *Bum Phillips*

CHAPTER FOUR:
Going for the Goal

Every sport has its grand prize – that elusive trophy for which every team strives. Perform well, and you drink from the cup. Otherwise, it's "better luck next year." But next year, it's still there, motivating players to run faster, push harder, jump higher or endure longer.

How do you make restaurant teams perform to the best of their abilities? You have to give them something to strive for by compensating for their performance as it relates to the team.

Team-building compensation is a whole different attitude in the restaurant industry. Servers are used to being tipped for individual performance and singled out for high sales while kitchen staff and management are often paid the same no matter how good their performance.

On the following pages, you'll learn how to encourage teamwork by rewarding staff for their participation in a team environment. These practical (and a few radical) ideas will help you motivate team members to "go for the goal," by tying their pay to the performance of the team.

47 Pay for Play

Team-based compensation

Rewarding people for their performance within the group is a new philosophy for restaurant operations. Servers are used to being tipped for their individual performances with guests, the rest often get paid the same no matter how good their performance.

It's a struggle trying to persuade employees that working cooperatively with others is in their best interest. It's even more difficult when you tell them they must forget a lifetime of seeking personal glory. But research has shown that when real teamwork is required to get the job done, team-based recognition can be a powerful motivator for effective team players.

Teams rewarded on a strictly team basis, with everybody sharing equally, almost always outperform teams in which certain persons are rewarded more than others.

Sounds great ... right? But not so fast. If you try to change pay systems *before* workers have firsthand experience with what it means to be a part of a team, they'll look at it and say, "This is unfair – I should be paid on what I do. I don't have any control over what those other people do."

Later on, after team members have discovered what it means to work closely in pursuit of a common goal, they may demand more equitable pay systems.

For restaurant teams, these non-traditional pay systems are a little easier to digest than in other industries. Our teams are permanent, ongoing work teams, rather than project teams where members may work on two or three different teams. In ongoing work teams, it's easier to attach dollars to goal achievements without one employee breaking the bank.

So begin thinking about bonuses for achieving goals. They must either be the same for everyone on the team, or percentage based. No secret envelopes.

And in an effort to encourage team members to become cross-trained, offer a base wage determined by an employee's primary skill and offer small salary boosts by learning new skills that will help them do other jobs on the team.

Base a team member's salary by determining the kind of job he or she holds. Reserve incentive pay – the variable pay part of the equation – for the team's tangible results.

TIP

A Team-Player Culture Is Developed

- Leaders emphasize the importance of team players – not just "teamwork."
- Managers serve as models of team players.
- Team-player behaviors are incorporated into performance review systems.
- Training workshops are provided to encourage team-player skills.
- Incentive systems are developed to reward team effort.
- Compensation programs are revised to pay individuals for their contributions to a team approach.
- A program of team awards is tailored to the needs of the organization.
- Managers use a variety of nonmonetary forms of recognition that appeal to intrinsic motivation.
- Competitive rating and ranking systems that do not value team-player contributions are eliminated.

48 Positive Feedback

Team-based performance appraisals

Constant feedback will show your employees where they stand – both with you and with their teammates. Regular employee performance reviews are great tools for communicating your expectations, setting goals and celebrating when goals have been achieved. They're also great opportunities to provide an employee with feedback from other members of the team. And they will help you avoid "aboutism" – team members talking among themselves about someone else's performance instead of confronting that person.

Before you do regular performance reviews, distribute a brief anonymous questionnaire to other members of the team. On the questionnaire, ask teammates questions about:

- *Relationships:* Is the employee friendly and approachable in and outside of the work group? Does he or she seem trustworthy?

- *Innovation:* Does he or she solve problems creatively? Does the employee seek and develop new ideas? Is the employee a force in improving processes?

- *Accountability:* Does the person hold him or herself responsible for actions? Does the employee take the initiative to identify and solve problems without blaming others?

- *Spirit:* Is he or she enthusiastic about the work? Does the employee excite others through example?

> **"Research shows time and time again that what employees want most is for their manager to tell them face to face they're doing a good job. Unfortunately, they most often hear from the boss when they've made a mistake."**
> — *Bob Nelson, author*

- *Flexibility:* Is the person responsive to unscheduled requests? Is he or she able to shift tasks and maintain priorities and adjust to changing situations without undue stress or complaint?

- *Teamwork:* Is this person a valued member of the team? Does he or she solicit help when needed? Does he or she contribute actively as a team member and inspire teamwork in others?

- *Initiative and drive:* Is he or she a self-starter, seeking out opportunities to influence events? Does the employee have a high energy level?

Ask a few essay-style questions, as well, so peers will be specific. Ask, "What kind of a worker is he?" and "Have you given that person any feedback on problem areas?" And guide the peer reviewer into thinking about solutions by asking, "What can the team do to help this person?"

Anonymity is the key to having peer reviews build – instead of break – teams. When you meet with the reviewee, don't read straight from the peer questionnaires. Just give them an overall picture of the comments. Use this time to discuss strengths and create a plan to improve areas that need work.

Constructive Criticism

Don't bend the rules and lower standards for one low-performing employee. Low standards produce low morale and decrease levels of performance throughout your operation. And that's no way to build teamwork. Here's how to effectively discipline an employee when you see a problem:

- **Discipline immediately.**
- **Be specific in explaining the problem.**
- **Focus on the performance problem, not the employee.**
- **Emphasize how the problem negatively affects the team and its goals.**
- **Ask for the employee's help in solving the problem.**
- **Reach an agreement and write it down.**
- **Express confidence in the employee's ability to solve the problem and offer praise with the first improvements.**

49 In the Bank

Compensation ideas for employees

> **"Money can't buy friends, but you can get a better class of enemy."**
> — *Spike Milligan*

In corporate America's new team-based culture, even salespeople – the most individual of occupations – are seeing changes in their compensation systems.

With many salespeople working on a single account, sales managers are finding that compensation must support and encourage teamwork while ensuring fair pay for each player.

Which raises an important question for restaurant operators who are trying to build a team culture: What if tips were pooled? If you're going to ask servers to work together as a team to serve each guest, why should just one server get to pocket that guest's generous tip?

We're not suggesting that you come in one day and tell selfish servers that now they'll have to share. You won't *actually* pool their tips.

But we are suggesting that you study the results of tip-pooling as a team-building exercise to show servers how helping each other makes everyone a little wealthier.

Go back to your "Buddy Teams" which combine lower-performing servers with selling superstars. For one week, have them focus on their section alone, without offering help to their "buddy" server's adjacent section. Remind them to keep track of their tips.

During the next week, encourage Buddy Teams to strive to serve each other's guests without neglecting those in their own section.

At the end of each night, add together the total tips earned by both servers and announce any changes. Chances are good that both servers will see an improvement over their weekly tip average.

TIP   Raising Objections

Servers' sheer resistance to the suggestion of pooling tips is a team-building training point you won't want to skip over. When they raise their objections, shift leaders should raise the issue, "We all say we're committed to a common goal ... we all agree on the obvious benefits of creating a team culture. But think about your reaction when you heard that teaming might hit you in your own wallet. You're all willing to share your work but not the wealth that comes along with it. Think about it."

50 A Pat on the Back

Recognition for a job well done

> "With so many ways to reward people, you may ask, 'How do I decide how to reward each person?' The answer is simple: Ask them."
>
> — *Michael LeBoeuf*

Fostering a team environment won't happen overnight. But you can speed up the process by recognizing team members for their continued efforts. There are so many ways to reward employees for consistently good behavior – and it's one of the easiest and least expensive ways to keep them striving for your operation's goals.

As you've learned throughout this book, you shouldn't single team members out by ranking them, but you do want to reinforce positive team behaviors and encourage the same in other members of the team.

So instead of ranking the employee, rate their *performance* against established criteria. That gives every team member an opportunity to become a top performer.

And when their performance deems it – say the employee consistently does his or her job well and helps out others on the team – recognize that employee with a pat on the back. Let him or her know you appreciate the continued efforts toward your operation's goals.

Here are some tips on rewarding employees.

Be timely and specific. To be effective, recognition needs to happen fast. If you wait weeks to say "well done," you won't have motivated the employee to repeat the behavior.

Keep a stash of movie passes to hand out on the floor when you catch an employee "doing his part" for the team. It's inexpensive, instantaneous and motivational.

Match the reward to the achievement. If an employee team solves a major business problem that saves the restaurant thousands of dollars, members should receive a reward that's a little more substantial than a reward for someone who, as a favor, comes into work on his or her day off.

And the Winner Is ...

Once a year, hold your own Academy Awards ceremony to recognize positive team players. Don't single out high sales averages, though. Come up with creative categories like "MVP," most improved performance on a team, most agreeable, best helping hand, etc. Have fun with the ceremony, making it as simple or elaborate as you wish. Send out invitations inviting the employees to bring a guest. Plan a menu for the big event. Post a list of the categories where employees can see it and explain the criteria for being nominated for each award. Establish an employee committee to select the winners. Create a statuette resembling the real "Oscar" for each winner and award a prize or gag gift that reflects the category being recognized.

51 Eyes on the Prize

Increasing sales with a team approach.

We mentioned that sales incentives can hamper your team-building efforts. But that doesn't mean you should do away with them completely. Just take a look at your sales incentives with a different view: Use a team approach.

Here are some tips on creating front-of-the-house team incentives and contests that get results:

Start with the end in mind. Determine your specific desired result before you begin. Then plan and set goals backward.

> **"The point of contest, incentive and recognition programs is that they make everyone feel that service and sales are his or her individual responsibility. That not only leads to better service for the customer, it also means higher morale for the staff."**
> — *Lauren O'Connell, Citicorp*

- Communicate that goal to your staff in terms they'll understand. If, for instance, you want to increase appetizer sales by 10 percent this month, don't tell them, "To achieve this goal, we must sell 1,200 more appetizers this month." Break it down for them: "If we just sell 40 more appetizers per day, 20 per shift – that's only two per section, per shift. We can easily achieve this goal."

- Don't set quotas – work together to set goals. If you tell members of the team to sell 10 desserts on their next shift, that's *your* goal, not *theirs*. Team "buy in" to your incentive or contest is critical to its success. Members must agree not only on how to achieve the goal, but also on what behavior is necessary to achieve the goal.

- Structure sales contests to generate several winners. Reward not only highest check average or highest-sales per hour, but also the most-improved sales percentage. This helps eliminate the "same-server-always-wins" syndrome. Post and update your check averages and sales results at least weekly, but preferably daily, and include each server's "personal best" high check average. Reward those who exceed their personal best every week.

- Post a contest board so the team can see its progress.

- Be creative in selecting prizes: Awards can include merchandise, gift certificates or simply praise in writing.

Motivating Buddy Teams

Give under-achieving salespeople a boost by pairing them with your top servers. It will promote front-of-the-house teamwork and show struggling servers how their peers go about their business. Start by evaluating sales averages for all your servers. Look at individual sales averages and sales averages by category to pair up the highest and the lowest performers. Choose a category to focus on – say, appetizer sales. Don't make a big deal about the reasons for the pairings. Just use your regular "Buddy System" to pair up teams in adjacent sections. Encourage them to buddy up before each shift, giving each other pep talks, sharing sales techniques and developing their own shift goals. During the shift, they should stop by tables in the other server's section to recommend appetizers. At the end of the contest, reward the winning pair with prizes worthy of the hard work they put in.

52 Go Team

Involve all of your teams in contests and incentives

> "I'd rather have an employee with half the academic credentials and twice the team spirit, because without that, you've got nothing."
>
> — *Stan Bentley, Diversified Systems Inc.*

Make all your incentive programs and contests team efforts. Every member of your restaurant's staff has a stake in the success of the operation. And every guest's order impacts all departments.

Think about it: Every item sold is prepared by a prep cook, dished up by a cook, and suggested to guests by servers, bartenders or greeters. The plate it's served on is cleared by a buser and washed by a dishwasher.

When you create incentives to encourage servers to increase sales, you're really asking everyone on staff to work doubly hard. Why would you only reward the server?

So before you go dreaming up another sales incentive for your servers, think about how that sale affects every other department in the restaurant.

Say you want to sell 1,200 more desserts this month. Your first step would be to identify everyone involved in the process of merchandising desserts to your guests. This list would include greeters, servers, bartenders, busers, cooks, prep cooks and managers.

Then ask yourself, "What's in it for the prep cooks to make better desserts?" "What's in it for the cooks to get the desserts out quickly?" "What's in it for the greeters to consistently suggest desserts to every guest they seat?" Granted, one could answer that "they get to keep their jobs," but if you're creating incentives and prizes for the waitstaff to sell more, remember that your kitchen staff may be thinking, "Why should I bust my butt when *they* win all the prizes?"

Here are some solutions: Prep cooks can be rewarded for zero mistakes in making the desserts. The kitchen crew can be rewarded for consistently getting them out under five minutes, for any shift when not a single serving gets wasted or for any shift when 60 or more are sold. When the front-of-the-house team reaches your desired goal of dessert sales, hand out awards to not only the servers, but the greeters, bartenders and busers who put in an extra effort to make suggestions to guests.

TIP

The Top 10 Ways To Reward Good Work

1. Money
2. Recognition
3. Time off
4. A piece of the action
5. Favorite work

6. Advancement
7. Freedom
8. Personal Growth
9. Fun
10. Prizes

Action Plan

To most effectively put these ideas to work for you, we suggest following these steps:

- Read the book cover to cover.

- Take notes and make a list of the ideas from each chapter that best apply to your operation.

- Give a copy of this book to all of your managers, assistant managers and shift leaders.

- Have them take notes and make lists of the ideas from each chapter that best apply to your operation.

- Schedule a meeting to discuss your operation's philosophies on building teamwork, training procedures and compensation policies.

- Prioritize the lists of ideas to develop a "Team Building Strategy," a "Planning Strategy," a "Staff Training Strategy" and a "Rewards Strategy."

- Assign a specific staffer to captain the implementation of each of the following Strategies.

Strategy One

- Prepare a mission statement for your operation. Set mission statements for individual teams. Prepare a list of tasks, by department, that will help you achieve the goal.

- Evaluate all polices and procedures, eliminating those that encourage the individual over the team. Write, or re-write employee handbooks.

- Review recruiting, hiring and interviewing procedures. Make changes accordingly.

- Choose shift team leaders and begin leadership training.

- Call a staff meeting to announce your team-building strategy. Read selections from this book, and solicit feedback. Pass out new employee handbooks and explain new policies.

Strategy Two

- Review job descriptions. Make changes to task and role descriptions accordingly.

- Evaluate scheduling procedures.

- Arrange meetings with each department to describe your vision of teamwork in their area.

- Review your own job description, outlining tasks that could be delegated to employee teams. Form those teams, and monitor their work.

Strategy Three

- Review staff training outlines.

- Evaluate current training process for orientation, pre-shift meetings, role-playing, cross-training and mentors.

- Schedule monthly training sessions on these topics:
    Open Communication
    Foreign Language (if necessary)
    Trust
    Commitment to the Goal
    Accountability
    Brainstorming

Strategy Four

- Evaluate current compensation plan for front of the house, kitchen and management.

- Revise performance appraisal process. Design peer questionnaire form.

- Develop team-based incentives, contests and awards.

Have It All!

Pencom International Presents <u>More</u> Ways for Your Team to Win

Invest in the rest of the series for managers that provides 52 ways — an idea a week — to increase profits and improve business.

The *52 Ways...* Series

Turn the Tables on Turnover: *52 Ways to Find, Hire & Keep the Best Hospitality Employees*

Find good employees, learn the right interview questions and discover how to keep your best employees. This best-selling book includes innovative recruiting strategies, leadership tips and action plan. (PUB-523) $19.95.

Pour It On: *52 Ways to Maximize Your Bar Profits*

Determine the right price for all your beverage items, out-*present* the competition, instead of out-*pricing* them, create fun marketing promotions that keep your guests coming back and teach your staff wine and hand-crafted beer basics. (PUB-540) $19.95.

Playing Games at Work: *52 Best Incentives, Contests & Rewards*

Improve sales, service and safety, build teamwork, increase product knowledge and reduce waste-watching — all with this book that motivates employees with some of the best incentives, contests and rewards! (PUB-520) $19.95.

Pump Up Your Profits: *52 Cost-Saving Ideas To Build Your Bottom Line*

Packed with hot tips, the information in this book will save you thousands in one year. Each tip is guaranteed to save you cash or your money back! (PUB-541) $19.95.

The *How To Sell More...* Series

The best way to make more money? Show your staff how to make it for you! You'll find that a little smart selling adds up to hundreds of additional dollars a day ... up to $25,000 to $100,000 a year, depending on the number of guests you serve daily!

How To Sell More Desserts video
Sell *more* desserts — and add literally thousands to your bottom line! This video teaches your staff how to raise check averages — and increase tips — with selling strategies for dessert trays, table tents, descriptive phrases and more. (TVC-32) $69.

How To Sell More Appetizers video
With more than 25 ways to sell more appetizers — at dinner and lunch — you're guaranteed to increase appetizer sales by 25 to 45 percent. (TVC-28) $69.

How To Sell More Wine video
When your servers know how to open, serve and recommend wine, you'll double your wine and champagne sales — by the bottle and the glass — and you'll upsell glasses to bottles and house brands to varietals. (TVC-29) $69.

How To Sell More Beer video
Double draft beer sales, move more non-alcohol brews and make 25 cents more profit off every beer you sell. (TVC-27) $69.

How To Sell More Premium Spirits video
Liquidate cocktails into cold hard cash when you upsell well drinks to call drinks seven out of 10 times. (TVC-30) $69.

How to Sell More... posters

Once you've taught your servers to think and act like salespeople, keep their training top-of-mind with these colorful, laminated posters.

10 Ways to Sell More Wine & Champagne (POS-101)
10 Ways to Sell More Appetizers (POS-102)
10 Ways to Sell More Beer (POS-103)
10 Ways to Sell More Summer Specialty Drinks (POS-104)
10 Ways to Sell More Margaritas (POS-105)
10 Ways to Sell More Premium Spirits (POS-107)
10 Ways to Sell More Desserts (POS-210)
$7.95 each or any five for $24.95.

Server Dialogue Cards

OK, it's a cheat-sheet. We admit it. These little cards (just 3" x 5") fit inside any order pad to give your servers the smart-selling tips they need — *when* they need them.

10 Ways to Sell More Wine & Champagne (SDC-101)
10 Ways to Sell More Appetizers (SDC-102)
10 Ways to Sell More Beer (SDC-103)
10 Ways to Sell More Summer Specialty Drinks (SDC-104)
10 Ways to Sell More Margaritas (SDC-105)
10 Ways to Sell More Premium Spirits (SDC-107)
10 Ways to Sell More Desserts (SDC-108)
Available in packs of 25 for $9.95.

It's easy. Just **call 1-800-247-8514** to order these products or for a **free catalog** of other Pencom International training and marketing solutions. Or fill out and mail in the order form on the next page.

I. ORDERED BY

Print name		Title
Company name		
Address (Please no P.O.Boxes)		This address is: ❑ Home ❑ Business
City	State	Zip
Telephone # (Required to process order)	Fax #	

2. SHIP TO *(IF DIFFERENT)*

Print name	Title	
Company name		
Address (Please no P.O.Boxes) ❑ Home ❑ Business		
City	State	Zip
Telephone # (Required)	Fax #	

3. METHOD OF PAYMENT

❑ I've enclosed check # _____ payable to Pencom, Inc.

❑ Please charge to the following credit card:

❑ American Express *(15 digits)*   ❑ Discover *(16 digits)*

❑ MasterCard *(16 digits)*   ❑ Visa *(13 or 16 digits)*

1	2	3	4	5	6	7	8	9	10	11	12	13	14	15	16

Expiration Date

Print Cardholder's Name

4. ORDER

Title	Quantity	Audio	Video	Unit Price	Total

5. SHIPPING AND HANDLING

Continental U.S.

❑ **Standard Two-Day Delivery via Airborne Express**

All orders for in-stock items are shipped within 24 hours after we receive your order. Most orders will be delivered within 2 days of shipment. Add $4.95 for the first item and $1.75 for each additional item.

❑ **Guaranteed Next Business Day Delivery via Airborne Express**

Orders for in-stock items received by noon MST will be shipped that day and delivered the next day. Orders received after 12 noon will be shipped the next day and delivered within 24 hours of shipment. Add $9.95 for the first item and $1.75 for each additional item.

Call For Rates Outside the Continental U.S.

Merchandise total	
Shipping & handling *(see left)*	
Subtotal	
Colorado residents *(add 7.3% sales tax)*	
Grand total	